EVERYDAY READING

GRAPHS, CHARTS, AND FORMS

EVERYDAY READING SERIES

AGS
PUBLISHING

Circle Pines, Minnesota 55014-1796
800-328-2560
www.agsnet.com

Publisher's Project Staff

Vice President, Product Development: Kathleen T. Williams, Ph.D., NCSP; Associate Director, Product Development: Teri Mathews; Editor: Judy Monroe; Assistant Editor: Sarah Brandel; Development Assistant: Bev Johnson; Creative Services Manager: Nancy Condon; Senior Designer: Daren Hastings; Project Coordinator/Designer: Laura Henrichsen; Desktop Production Artist: Peggy Vlahos; Materials Management: Carol Nelson; Marketing Director: Brian Holl

Development and writing services by Ellen McPeek Glisan

© 2004 AGS Publishing
4201 Woodland Road, Circle Pines, MN 55014-1796
800-328-2560 • www.agsnet.com

AGS Publishing is a trademark and trade name of American Guidance Service, Inc.

Printed in the United States of America

Product Number 92140
ISBN 0-7854-3675-8

A 0 9 8 7 6 5 4 3 2 1

CONTENTS

Introduction

Reading is a part of every day in the world around you. Reading is like anything else that matters. To be good at it, you have to practice. *Everyday Reading: Graphs, Charts, and Forms* will help you be a better reader. You will learn how to read information that is given in different ways.

What is a **graph, chart** or **form**? Graphs, charts, and forms are ways to show information without using sentences. They are also called tables, webs, or maps. Graphs, charts, and forms often use columns or rows. Sometimes they use bars, circles, boxes, or pictures. In all cases, they show a lot of information that can be understood with little reading.

You will see graphs, charts, and forms in textbooks, newspapers, magazines, and other places. Learn to read them so you can get a lot of information fast.

Here are the graphs, charts, and forms you will use in this book:

■ **Bar Graphs**
Can you read lots of information in one glance? You can if the details are given in a bar graph!

■ **Pie Charts**
Pie charts aren't for dessert—they are to show how pieces of a whole relate to each other. Learn to read pie charts, and you can learn a lot with a quick look.

■ **Sports Statistics**
Have you ever wanted to know about a sporting event that you missed? Lots of people do, and sports statistics make it possible. Sports statistics sum up a whole game in a few inches of space.

■ **Information Maps**
Information maps are made up of connected circles or squares. They can lay out a story, or a meal plan, or show a bus route. You read them by following the circles or squares.

■ **Size Charts**
Many different size plans are used for clothes. If you can read a size chart, you can figure out the size you need.

■ **Telephone Bills**
Telephone bills are made by computers. The details are printed in a chart. Read your telephone bill so you know you are paying the right amount.

■ Utility Bills

Utility bills often include charts and graphs. The charts and graphs tell how much the bill is for and other facts.

■ Forms

A form is any written information that has blanks to fill in. Forms can include charts, graphs, webs, tables, or text.

■ Information Charts

Information charts usually have top headings and side headings. By following the headings, you can read groups of facts.

■ Tables

Tables are columns of numbers. It isn't usually important to read all the numbers. The main thing is to find the numbers you need.

■ Comparison Charts

Comparison charts show how two or more things relate to each other. One example is the services at different parks.

■ Stock Market Reports

Most newspapers include a list of stock market numbers. These numbers tell how much stocks are selling for that day. If you ever buy stock, you can watch the prices change over time.

PERSONAL READING GOALS

Set goals for yourself before you start this book. At the end of the book, come back to see how you did with your goals.

I want to learn more about _____

_____

_____

One thing in reading I want to be better at by the end of this book is

_____

_____

_____

READING STRATEGIES

In this book, you will use reading strategies, reading comprehension skills, and critical thinking tools. You will learn to look at reading from different points of view. Here are some tips and strategies you can use to get started.

Word Study: Five Steps to Learning a Word

1. **Read the word.** Notice its shape. Is it long or short? What letters does it begin with? Does it look like other words you know?

2. **Say the word.** What sounds does it have? Which letters stand for those sounds?

3. **Write the word.** Get a feel for the word by writing it down.

4. **Practice reading the word.** Read the word again and again until you know it.

5. **Use the word.** Add the word to your vocabulary, both when you speak and when you write.

Spelling Tips

Use these tips to help you spell correctly when you write:

- **Listen to the sounds.** Listen for the sounds you hear at the beginning, in the middle, and at the end of a word.

- **Think about letters.** Ask yourself: What letters or letter patterns usually stand for the sounds in this word?

- **Think about meaning.** Should you write **hair** or **hare**? Is the word you want spelled **won** or **one**? Thinking about how the word is used in a sentence helps you know which spelling to use.

- **Picture the word.** Make a mental picture of the word. Think about its shape and length.

- **Check the word.** Look at the word after you've written it. Does it look right? If you're not sure, look in a dictionary.

Word Attack Tips

Most short words are simple to read. When you come to longer words, it's easy to get stumped. Here are some tips that can help:

- **Look for word parts you know.** Is the word made up of a smaller word you know, plus an ending?

- **Look for letter patterns you know.** Knowing a pattern of letters can help you read other words with that pattern. If you can read **main,** then you are reading the **ain** letter pattern. This means you can also read **train, brain, stained,** and **raining**.

- **Break the word into parts.** Is the word made up of two smaller words that have been put together?

- **Look for syllables.** The vowels in a word are a clue to how many syllables (parts) it has.

- **Look at the letters in the word.** What sounds do the letters stand for? Blend all the sounds together to read the word.

Reading Strategies

A strategy is a smart plan for getting a job done. Reading strategies help with the job of reading. Here are some strategies you'll learn to use:

- **Preview and predict.** Looking ahead at your reading can help you know what to expect.

- **Set a purpose.** Every time you read, you do it for a reason. Knowing that reason can help you understand what you read.

- **Think critically.** Reading without thinking is like chewing without swallowing. What's the point? This book will show you how to think about what you read by asking yourself questions.

- **Use things you already know.** You probably know something about most things you read. Try to think about these things before you read. It makes reading more interesting.

- **Read actively.** When you are active, reading is more fun. This book will teach you to mark text, take notes, and ask questions.

Lesson

1

BEFORE READING

Part-Time Job

Below are three common silent letters. The slashed letter is silent.

b̸t as in debt
d̸ as in edge
h̸ as in exhibit

VOCABULARY

bar graph
a graph that uses bars to show numbers

data
numbers

graph
to show a relationship between pieces of information using bars, lines, or parts of a circle

horizontal
parallel to the horizon

part-time
working less than 40 hours in a week

vertical
straight up and down, upright

visual
of sight, by sight

Letters and Sounds

Read the words in the box. Then write them where they belong below.

honor hedge made	subtle exhaust undo	hear mishap heir	doubt handkerchief obtain

b̸t	d̸	h̸
1. _____	3. _____	5. _____
2. _____	4. _____	6. _____
		7. _____

bt	d	h
8. _____	9. _____	11. _____
	10. _____	12. _____

Use What You Know

A bar graph shows numbers in a visual way. Bar graphs help you understand and compare numbers. Answer the questions below about bar graphs.

1. Have you ever seen a bar graph in a book, newspaper, or magazine? Circle one.   Yes   No   If yes, what information did it show?

   _____

   _____

2. Have you ever made a bar graph? Circle one.   Yes   No   If yes, what information did it show? _____

   _____

3. Why do you think a bar graph can be easier to read than a paragraph?

   _____

   _____

READING Part-Time Job

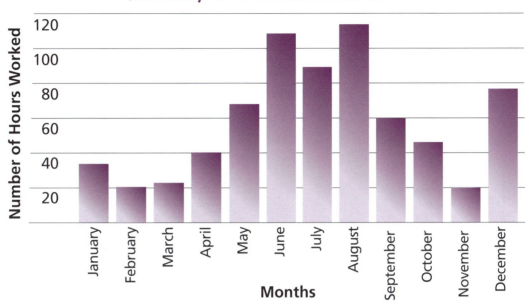

Number of Hours Worked by Mia, January to December 2005

Bar Graphs

A **bar graph** uses bars to show numbers in a **visual** way. Every bar graph has these four parts:

- ■ a title which tells the topic of the bar graph
- ■ a **horizontal** line with a label
- ■ a **vertical** line with a label
- ■ **data** shown in bars

To understand a bar graph, follow the steps below.

1. Read the title.
2. Read the headings across the bottom and on the left side. The headings tell the information shown on that side of the graph.
3. Read the height of each bar by following each bar to its highest point.

The bar graph above tells the:

- ■ title—the number of hours Mia worked each month in 2005. Mia works **part-time**.
- ■ horizontal line—the twelve months of the year
- ■ vertical line—the number of hours worked each month, from 0 to 120 hours. For example, Mia worked 40 hours in April 2005.

Lesson **1**

AFTER READING

Part-Time Job

STRATEGY

Context Clues is a reading strategy. It uses all parts on a page such as words, graphs, and text. Use these parts to help you figure out unknown words.

READING COMPREHENSION

Sometimes you need to think about details to understand what you see.

LIFE SKILLS

Graphs, charts, and other graphic aids show information. Visual aids help you see and compare things. They also help you understand and see what words tell about.

Reading Comprehension

Read the bar graph on page 9. Then answer the questions below.

1. **Use Context Clues:** The bar graph shows what data?

_____

2. **Understand:** What three months have the tallest bars?

_____

Why do you think these bars are taller than the other nine months?

_____

_____

3. **Read for Details:** During what two months did Mia work the least number of hours?

_____

4. **Make a Chart:** Curtis made a bar graph of the hours he worked last week. Study his bar graph below. Then add his Saturday hours where they belong. Color the bar so it shows a height of 6 hours.

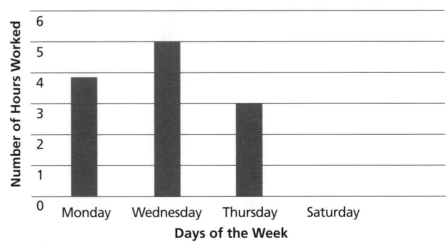

Number of Hours Worked by Curtis: Monday, Wednesday, Thursday, and Saturday

Read the sentences below. Then circle each word that has one of these silent letters: bt, d, or h.

1. Christine likes crackers and milk.

2. The shepherd came home with the sheep.

3. Thomas left his coat in the boathouse.

4. I doubt that we will see the bobtail deer near the hedge.

5. Theresa wore her blue dress.

6. He has a lot of debt because of bad habits.

7. It is not honest to take the horn.

8. The car has an exhaust problem.

9. Anna put a plant on the wide ledge.

LIFE SKILLS

Bar graphs are easy to read. They show how information compares quickly.

Language

Read the compound sentences below. Then add the missing commas.

1. Most garden shops are busy in the summer but they are slower in the winter.

2. Cam wanted to buy potato plants in January but no shop sold them.

3. I will plant this bush or I will pay someone to plant it.

4. I will buy a new bike or I will buy a used bike.

5. I took the tree back and I bought some flowers.

6. I will plant the flowers now or I will plant them tomorrow.

7. Eric works at Toni's store part-time but he wants a new job.

8. Eric likes his job but he wants to work more hours in the winter.

9. Toni does not want Eric to go but she understands.

10. Chow wants to work at the store and he will talk to Toni.

LANGUAGE

A **compound sentence** is two small sentences put together. A word such as **and, or,** or **but** connects the two small sentences. Use a comma before **and, or,** or **but**.

Examples:
- The dog slept, and the cat played.
- Ethan stayed, but Lauren came along.
- Maria will come with us, or she will ride with Bo.

One of the costs of driving to work in a city is parking. The table below lists the costs for one hour of parking in five parking lots. Use the information in the table to draw a bar graph.

1. Read the data in the table.

Cost for One Hour in a Parking Lot	
Manny's Park	$2.00
Town Parking	$3.75
Grand Town Park	$3.25
Park Here	$2.50
Park and Save	$1.00

2. Make a bar graph of the information. Write the names of the parking lots across the bottom of the bar graph. Write the costs along the left side. Make bars and fill them in. Write a title and labels for the horizontal and vertical lines. For ideas, see the bar graphs on pages 9 and 10.

Title:_____

2 BEFORE READING   Your Own Bar Graph

Word Skills

Read the word before each sentence. Then add the prefix pre or dis to each word. Write the new words where they belong below.

1. (belief) DaWayne looked at me in _____.

2. (heat) Make sure you _____ the oven.

3. (color) My shirt started to _____ right away.

4. (able) Let's _____ the heater until it is fixed.

5. (cover) Erin didn't _____ the problem until it was too late.

6. (owned) I bought a _____ car.

7. (obeyed) The puppy _____ and ran away.

Use What You Know

Find a bar graph in a newspaper, a magazine, an almanac, or on the Internet. Tape, staple, or glue the bar graph to page 14. Then answer the questions below.

1. Where did you find your bar graph?

_____

2. Read the title of the bar graph. What kind of information do you think your bar graph will show?

_____

_____

READING   Your Own Bar Graph

Find a bar graph in a newspaper, a magazine, an almanac, or on the Internet. Tape, staple, or glue the bar graph to this page.

Lesson
2

AFTER READING

Your Own Bar Graph

READING COMPREHENSION

You often use the information you read to build on other ideas.

READING COMPREHENSION

Reading comprehension uses three types of activities:

■ **Reading Strategies** A strategy is a smart plan for getting a job done.

■ **Reading Comprehension Skills** Use these skills to help make facts you read stick.

■ **Critical Thinking Tools** Ask yourself questions as you read. This will hep you think about what your read.

You will learn more about these tools in this book.

Reading Comprehension

Read your bar graph on page 14. Then answer the questions below.

1. **Use Context Clues:** Choose one word you do not know. Fill in the box below to help you learn the meaning of the word.

> **Word I do not know** _____
>
> Helpful words in the same sentence or phrase _____
>
> Helpful sentence or phrase before the word _____
>
> Helpful sentence or phrase after the word _____
>
> **What does the word mean?** _____
>
> _____
>
> _____

2. **Understand:** Why do you think a bar graph was used to show the information?

_____

_____

_____

3. **Read for Details:** Look for a piece of information that someone may not see right away. Write the information on the lines below.

_____

_____

_____

4. **Draw a Picture:** On your own paper, draw, glue, or tape something that goes with your graph. Write why you chose this piece of information.

Language Review

On your own paper, write three compound sentences that use the items below.

- the word **and**
- the word **but**
- the word **or**

Do not add punctuation when you write your sentences. Then trade sentences with a classmate. Add punctuation to each other's sentences.

WRITING

Write a title, horizontal line, and vertical line labels when you make bar graphs. This information makes your bar graph easier to understand.

Writing

Make a bar graph of the time you spent on homework last week.

1. Write the number of minutes you spent on homework each day last week in the table below.

Number of Minutes on Homework	
Sunday	
Monday	
Tuesday	
Wednesday	
Thursday	
Friday	
Saturday	

2. On your own paper, make a bar graph to show this information. To do this, write the days of the week across the bottom. Write the minutes on the left side. Make and fill in rectangular bars. Write a title. Write labels for the horizontal and vertical lines.

Career Connection

Read the two lists below. Draw a line from each type of bar graph to the work place that uses it. Some bar graphs can match more than one work place.

Bar Graphs	Work Places
1. Sales for workers	Movie store
2. Number of books checked out each month	Hospital
3. Car sales each month	Computer company
4. Babies born each month	Cleaning company
5. Cost of cleaning supplies	Library
6. New movies rented each week	Office supply company
7. Overtime hours for workers	Car sales store or dealership

Lesson
3

BEFORE READING

Movie Choices

PHONICS

Below are three common silent letter pairs. The slashed letter is silent.

g̸h as in night
wh̸ as in why
p̸b as in cupboard

VOCABULARY

badge
a small piece of plastic, cloth, or metal that shows someone's status or belonging to a group

debt
money owed

decade
ten years

graham
whole wheat

handsome
beautiful, nice looking

pepper
a food flavoring made from the dried berry of an East Indian plant

raspberry
a black or red berry made up of small pieces, each with a seed inside

subtle
delicate, highly skillful

Letters and Sounds

Look at Pie Chart 1 on page 19. Find and write the following words on the lines below.

1. Two words with b̸t like in **doubt**

_____   _____

2. A word with d̸g as in **edge**_____

3. Two words with h̸ like in **honest**

_____   _____

4. A word with g̸h like in **night**_____

5. A word with wh̸ like in **why** _____

6. A word with p̸b like in **cupboard** _____

Use What You Know

Answer the questions below.

1. Drama and comedy are two movie types. Write three other movie types.

_____

_____

_____

2. What are two of your favorite movie types?

_____

_____

3. What do think is the most favorite movie type in the United States?

_____

READING Movie Choices

1—Top Movies for the Week

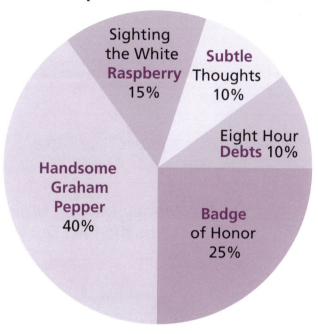

Sighting the White **Raspberry** 15%

Subtle Thoughts 10%

Eight Hour **Debts** 10%

Handsome Graham Pepper 40%

Badge of Honor 25%

2—Top Actress Roles for the Past **Decade**

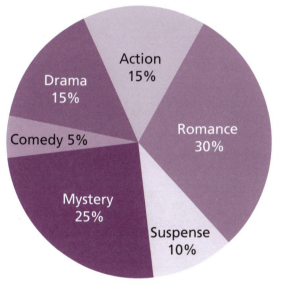

Action 15%

Drama 15%

Comedy 5%

Romance 30%

Mystery 25%

Suspense 10%

3—Top Actor Roles for the Past Decade

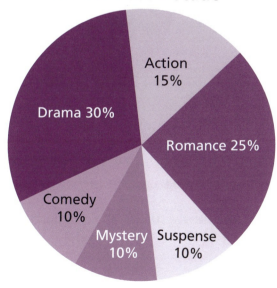

Action 15%

Drama 30%

Romance 25%

Comedy 10%

Mystery 10%

Suspense 10%

Understanding Pie Charts

You can get most information you need by just looking at a pie chart. To understand a pie chart, follow the steps below.

1. Read the title. It tells you what the chart is measuring.
2. Read the slices of information in the pie chart. The bigger the piece, the more it represents.

Lesson **3**

AFTER READING

Movie Choices

Reading Comprehension

Read the three pie charts on page 19. Then answer the questions below.

1. **Sum It Up:** What two movie types could make someone a top actor?

   _____

   What two movie types could make someone a top actress?

   _____

2. **Solve This:** Read the pie chart on the right. Then look at Pie Charts 2 and 3 on page 19. In the last decade, what are the three top movies types for picture, actor, and actress?

   _____

   _____

   _____

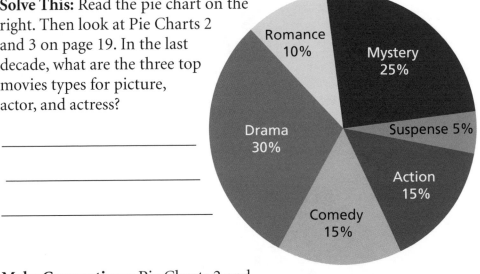

Top Money Making Movie Types for the Past Decade

3. **Make Connections:** Pie Charts 2 and 3 on page 19 show six types of movies. On your own paper, write the six types of movies. Then write a current movie title to match each movie type.

4. **Picture This:** Choose one movie title from Item 3 above. Think of how the title could be written at the beginning of the movie. On your own paper, draw your idea.

LANGUAGE

An **adjective** is a word that describes (tells about) a noun. Below are examples of adjectives.

- It's a **long, lazy** Saturday.

- Rashia lives in the **blue** house.

- Susan has lived in **four** cities.

- They had **some** time before the game started.

Read the clues below. All the words in the puzzle use words with these silent letter sets: b̶l̶, d̶, h̶, g̶h̶t, m̶b̶, and b̶b. Write each word in the puzzle.

Across
1. Not left
3. Full name for Tom
7. Nice looking man
8. A sheriff wears a _____.
9. To not believe

Down
2. Today I teach, Yesterday I _____
4. Large hammer
5. Where the plates are kept
6. What time

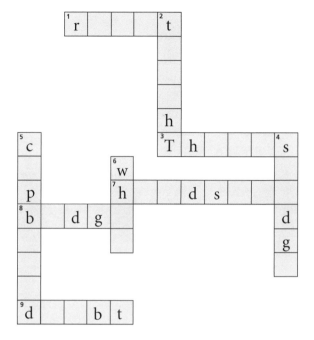

LANGUAGE

Use a comma between two adjectives that describe the same noun.

- Carlos saw a **large, red** fish jump out of the water.

Do not use a comma between two adjectives that describe different nouns.

- Ellie wore an **old leather** cap.

Old describes the **leather,** not the cap. So, no comma goes between old and leather.

Language

Add the missing commas to the sentences below. Then circle the adjectives that tell about the nouns.

1. Talia has curly brown hair and dark blue eyes.

2. The new down pillows are plump and soft.

3. Jan wore a light green dress and shiny black shoes.

On your own paper, write the sentences below. Then add one adjective and a comma to describe each noun in bold.

4. Matt likes to watch action **movies**.

5. When he watches movies, DeWayne eats buttered **popcorn**.

6. Marcus puts his popcorn into a large **bowl** and a small **cup**.

MAKING PIE CHARTS

You don't always need to figure out percentages when making a pie chart. To make the pie chart to the right:

1. Divide the circle into ten equal slices. The ten slices equal the total number of movies.

2. Group the slices together. In this pie chart, 3 movies are comedies so 3 slices are grouped together.

3. Write labels for all the pie slices.

4. Write a title for the pie chart.

LIFE SKILLS

People enjoy many types of movies. Favorites are comedy, drama, romance, action, drama, mystery, science fiction, musicals, and more. Some movies are made for children. Some movies combine two or more types such as comedy and romance.

Alike and Different: Read the Making Pie Charts box on the left. It tells you how to make the pie chart below. When making pie charts, be sure the percentages add up to 100 percent.

1. Read the data in the table. Then look at the pie chart below. Some of the data from the table has been put into the pie chart. Complete the pie chart.

Top Money Making Movie Types: Week of July 28	
Action—2 movies (20%)	Mystery—1 movie (10%)
Comedy—3 movies (30%)	Romance—1 movie (10%)
Drama—2 movies (20%)	Suspense—1 movie (10%)

Title: _____

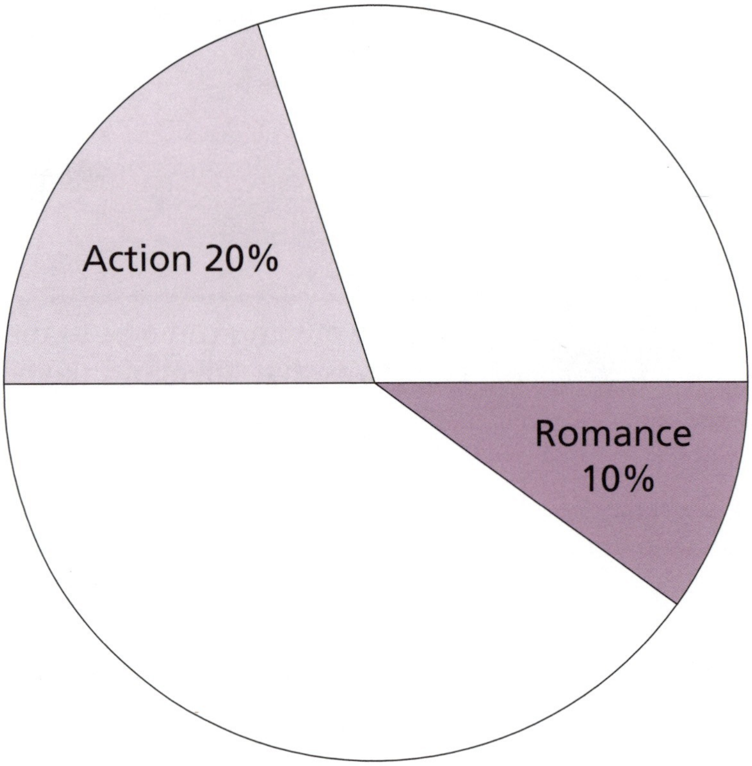

2. Look at the pie chart on page 20. Write the two top money making movie types for the past decade here.

_____

_____

3. Now look at the pie chart above. Is the top money making movie type on page 20 the same or different than the top one on this page? Circle one.   Same   Different

Lesson **4** **BEFORE READING**   **Your Own Pie Chart**

WORD SKILLS

A **suffix** is a word part added to the ending of a base word.

The suffix **ion** turns verbs into nouns. Below are two common patterns when adding the suffix **ion**.

act + ion = action

locate − e + ion = location

Word Skills

Add the suffix ion to each word below. Write the new word on the line. Then draw a picture of the new word in each box.

1. connect _____

3. subtract _____

2. graduate _____

4. vacate _____

Use What You Know

Find a pie chart in a newspaper, newspaper, book, or on the Internet. Tape, staple, or glue the pie chart to page 24. Then answer the questions below.

1. Read the title of your pie chart. What do you think your pie chart is

about? _____

_____

2. Find out what types of information are in the pie charts your classmates used. Tell about two of the pie charts below.

_____

_____

_____

Find a pie chart in a newspaper, book, or on the Internet.
Tape, staple, or glue the pie chart to this page.

Lesson 4 **AFTER READING**

Your Own Pie Chart

CRITICAL THINKING

Try to see something in your mind. You may "see" many details.

Reading Comprehension

Read the pie chart on page 24. Then answer the questions below.

1. **Sum It Up:** Tell about the pie chart in one or two sentences below.

_____

_____

_____

2. **Alike and Different:** Think about how bar graphs and pie charts are alike and different. See pages 9 and 14 for bar graphs. See pages 19 and 24 for pie charts. Write your answers below.

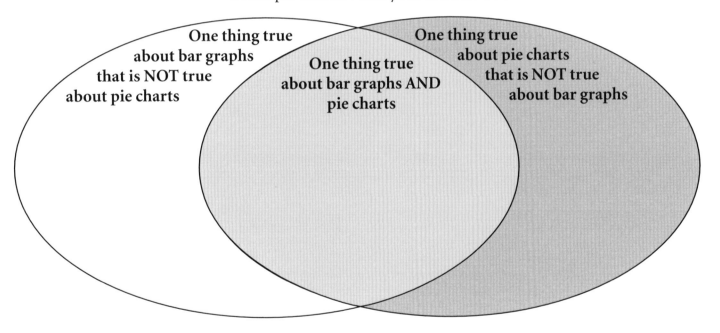

One thing true about bar graphs that is NOT true about pie charts

One thing true about bar graphs AND pie charts

One thing true about pie charts that is NOT true about bar graphs

3. **Make Connections:** Write one thing the pie chart on page 24 that has to do with you. _____

_____

4. **Picture This:** Picture a person making the pie chart on page 24. What are three items the person would need to make the pie chart?

_____

_____

Language Review

On your own paper, write four sentences that use the items below.

- the word **and**
- the word **but**
- a comma between two adjectives that tell about the same noun
- two adjectives that do not tell about the same noun

When you write your sentences, do not add the punctuation. Then trade your sentences with a classmate. Add punctuation to each other's sentences.

Writing

Choose a movie title from page 19 or Item 3 on page 20. In the space below, write story ideas to go with the title. On your own paper, write a short story. Write one or two paragraphs.

When you are done, proofread your short story. Make any changes. Then trade with a classmate and proofread each other's stories. Get your story back and make any changes. Write a final short story.

_____

_____

_____

_____

_____

_____

_____

_____

_____

_____

_____

_____

_____

_____

Pie charts show facts. These facts are found through research.

Career Connection

Eli wants to make a pie chart to show how students got to work in 2004. He put together the table below. Read the data in the table. Then make a pie chart below.

How Students Got to Work, 2004	
Carpool in car, truck, or van	20%
Drive alone in car, truck, or van	55%
Use public transportation	10%
Walk	10%
Other	5%

Title: _____

Lesson 5

BEFORE READING

Northwest Hockey Conference

PHONICS

Two common silent letter patterns are listed below. The slashed letter is silent.

w/h as in who
/t at end as in ballet

VOCABULARY

conference
a group of athletic teams

goal
a point scored by sending the puck into the net

goalie
guards the net

hockey
a game played on ice by two teams of six who try to get the puck into the other team's goal

loss
a game in which one team scores less points

opportunity
a good chance

period
one third of the length of one game

power play
a penalty time when one team has more players on the ice

Letters and Sounds

Read the words in the box. Write the words where they belong below. Then circle the silent letters.

habit who Wednesday raspberry	what whole behind ballet	hoghouse debt Rodney buffet	taught honor bobtail depot	upbringing whose warthog craft

Words with Silent Letters	11. _____
1. _____	12. _____
2. _____	**Words Without Silent Letters**
3. _____	13. _____
4. _____	14. _____
5. _____	15. _____
6. _____	16. _____
7. _____	17. _____
8. _____	18. _____
9. _____	19. _____
10. _____	20. _____

Use What You Know

Answer the questions below.

1. Have you ever played hockey or watched a hockey game? Circle one.
   Yes   No

   If yes, write a sentence about it._____

   _____

2. Write two sports that have statistics in your local newspaper.

   _____

READING   Northwest Hockey Conference

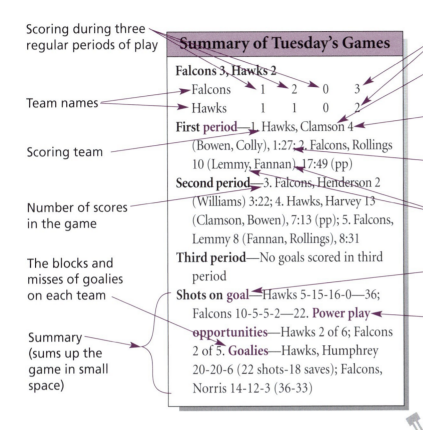

Scoring during three regular periods of play

Team names

Scoring team

Number of scores in the game

The blocks and misses of goalies on each team

Summary (sums up the game in small space)

Final score

Player who scored

Number on the shirt of the player who scored

Amount of time after the game started that the score was made

Players who helped with the score

Number of times each team tries to score

Because of a penalty (player broke rule and has to sit out), one team is short one or more players. This team has less chance to score.

Summary of Tuesday's Games

Falcons 3, Hawks 2

| Falcons | 1 | 2 | 0 | 3 |
| Hawks | 1 | 1 | 0 | 2 |

First period—1. Hawks, Clamson 4 (Bowen, Colly), 1:27; 2. Falcons, Rollings 10 (Lemmy, Fannan), 17:49 (pp)

Second period—3. Falcons, Henderson 2 (Williams) 3:22; 4. Hawks, Harvey 13 (Clamson, Bowen), 7:13 (pp); 5. Falcons, Lemmy 8 (Fannan, Rollings), 8:31

Third period—No goals scored in third period

Shots on goal—Hawks 5-15-16-0—36; Falcons 10-5-5-2—22. **Power play opportunities**—Hawks 2 of 6; Falcons 2 of 5. **Goalies**—Hawks, Humphrey 20-20-6 (22 shots-18 saves); Falcons, Norris 14-12-3 (36-33)

Northwest Hockey Conference

Team	W	L	T	OL	Pts	GF	GA
Dryden	42	9	5	4	93	227	133
Falcons	37	13	6	1	81	193	144
Wilson	35	15	4	4	78	150	113
Griggs	33	14	8	2	76	176	127
Hudson	30	16	11	2	73	136	125
Smithson	27	23	6	2	62	158	162
Stockton	24	26	4	5	57	153	170
W. Falls	23	30	7	2	55	157	189
Dumont	18	29	7	6	49	129	172
Lowell	13	38	5	3	34	132	204

Key: Wins, Losses, Overtime Losses, Points, Goals For, Goals Against

Two points for a win, one point for a tie, one point for an overtime loss

Tuesday's Games

Griggs 2, Smithson 5

Falcons 3, Hawks 2,

Today's Games

Griggs at Hawks, 6pm

Falcons at Dumont, 7pm

Lowell at Smithson, 7:00 pm

Dryden at W. Falls, 7:30 pm

Tuesday's Summary
Griggs 2, Smithson 5

| Griggs | 1 | 1 | 0—2 |
| Smithson | 3 | 1 | 1—5 |

First period—1. Smithson, Rivera 1 (Stone, Hengst), 7:35; 2. Smithson, Peterson 12 (Stone, Reiner), 14:49; 3. Smithson, Rivera 1 (Hengst, Rivera), 18:36; 4. Griggs, Norwash 15 (Scheele, VanDone), 19:48 pp

Second period—5. Griggs, Nash 16 (Scheele, Meshins), 2:55; 6. Smithson, Bellows 13 (Johnson, Garcia) 17.21

Third period—7. Smithson, Johnson 18 (Bellows, Garcia) 13:33

Shots on goal—Griggs 4-7-5—16; Smithson 15-7-13—35. Power play opportunities—Griggs 2 of 7; Smithson 1 of 8. Goalies—Griggs, Ariens 21-29-6 (35 shots-30 saves); Smithson, Hanson 13-15-6 (16-14)

Northwest Hockey Conference

STRATEGY

Study Text Features is a reading strategy. Use it to make a reading piece clear. Details are important in many things you read such as in sports statistics.

READING COMPREHENSION

If you don't understand what you read in the newspaper, ask someone for help.

Reading Comprehension

Read the hockey statistics on page 29. Then answer the questions below.

1. **Study Text Features and Make It Clear:** Look at the summary of Tuesday's games. Tell why the semicolon (;) is used.

   _____

   _____

   _____

2. **Think Further:** Sets of numbers and names are in each Tuesday summary, such as: 1. Smithson, Rivera 1 (Stone, Hengst) 7:35. Tell what each piece means below. If you do not know, talk to someone who understands hockey.

A 1.	
B Smithson,	
C Rivera	
D 1	
E (Stone, Hengst)	
F 7:35	

3. **Author's Purpose:** Sports statistics are written without directions for understanding all the parts. Why are sports statistics written this way?

   _____

   _____

4. **Brainstorm:** On your own paper, write four things hockey players use. Then write four skills someone needs to play hockey.

Letters and Sounds Review

Read the clues below. All the words in the puzzle use silent letters.
Write each word in the puzzle.

Across
3. To find in pounds
5. Even though
7. A train station
8. Healthy and good
9. Rim
10. Fits very closely

Down
1. The color of snow or salt
2. Toe dancing
3. ___ did the bell ring?
4. Quiet, fine, delicate
6. Always tells the truth

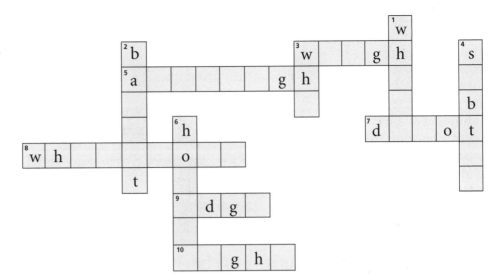

Language

Add the missing commas to the sentences below. To review about using commas, see the Language boxes on pages 11 and 21.

1. He threw away the broken red hockey stick.

2. Pedro is our goalie and he often has the hardest job.

3. The hockey field is down a long winding road.

4. Some people do not like hockey but Andy loves to play.

5. The team played overtime and they won the game.

6. Martina wants to see a hockey game or she wants to see a baseball game.

7. Bach wants to play hockey but she is a slow shaky skater.

8. Nigel skates well but he does not play hockey.

9. Latisha was amazed at the strong fast team.

10. Sports games have some wild crazy fans.

Other people besides sports writers write sports statistics. For example, an editor or a writer for a local newspaper may write about the area's sports. Parents sometimes give kids' sports information to newspapers. Knowing how to write sports statistics can help you understand sports.

Life Skills Focus

Put Steps in Order: Say that you work for a newspaper. Your job is to write the statistics about a hockey game. Follow the steps below.

1. Look at page 29 to figure out what type of information you need to gather.

2. Get information about a hockey game. To do this, do one or all of these:

   ■ Go to a hockey game or watch a hockey game on TV. Write down all the statistics you can during the game.

   ■ Read a newspaper or magazine article about a hockey game.

   ■ Read about a hockey game on the Internet.

3. Organize the information you need.

4. In the space below, write the statistics for the hockey game. Follow the format on page 29. If you are missing some information, write the word **unknown**.

BEFORE READING

Your Own Sports Statistics

Word Skills

Match a word from Box A with a prefix or suffix from Box B. Then write the new word to complete each sentence below.

A	discuss	attend	school	like	B	pre
	act	express	cook	pleased		dis
	react	locate	heat	own		ion

1. Mr. Hue from the zoo showed the little kids in _____ some snakes. Then he led a _____ about snakes.

2. I _____ seeing such a sad _____ on her face.

3. Dana was _____ that she forgot to _____ the meat.

4. Darin had given his homework little _____.
   His teacher had a bad _____ to that.

5. Get up and walk around. A little _____ will help you.

6. I thought she would _____ us and not talk to us again.

7. I don't know the room number. Do you know the _____ of the meeting?

8. Before you start making the cake, turn the oven to _____.

Use What You Know

Find statistics on any sport in a newspaper or magazine, or on the Internet. Tape, staple, or glue the statistics to page 34. Then answer the questions below.

1. What sport did you choose? _____

2. Why did you choose that sport? _____

   _____

3. How many of your classmates choose your sport? _____

Lesson 6

READING Your Own Sports Statistics

Find statistics on any sport in a newspaper or magazine, or on the Internet. Tape, staple, or glue the statistics to this page.

Lesson **6**   **AFTER READING**   **Your Own Sports Statistics**

Reading Comprehension

Read the sports statistics on page 34. Then answer the questions below.

1. Study Text Features and Make It Clear: Write three different text features used in the statistics. Tell why each feature was used.

Feature 1 _____

Why used_____

Feature 2 _____

Why used_____

Feature 3 _____

Why used_____

2. Think Further: Write two sentences that tell about a player who did well in the game. Also, tell what the player did to stand out.

_____

_____

_____

_____

_____

3. Put Steps in Order: Tell about the order used for some of the statistics.

_____

_____

_____

4. Brainstorm: On your own paper, write four things players use in this sport. Then write four skills someone needs to play this sport.

Language Review

On your own paper, write four sentences that use the items below.

- the word **and**
- the word **but**
- a comma between two adjectives that tell about the same noun
- one sentence with two adjectives that do not tell about the same noun

When you write your sentences, do not add the punctuation. Then trade with a classmate. Add punctuation to each other's sentences.

WRITING

Use active writing, or active voice, when you write. In active voice, the action in the sentence is always done by the subject of the sentence. Writing that is not active is called passive.

Active: Jane ran a good race.

Passive: A good race was run by Jane.

Writing

Write a short story about a sports activity below. Write one or two paragraphs and use active voice. When you are done, proofread your writing. Make any changes. If needed, use more paper.

_____

_____

_____

_____

_____

_____

_____

_____

_____

_____

_____

_____

_____

_____

Career Connection

Brainstorm: Many people work in sports. Below is a list of some sports jobs.

1. Choose one of the jobs below and circle it.

athlete	sports writer
coach	trainer
athletic director	announcer

2. Think about the good and bad parts of the job you chose above. Write your ideas about the good and bad parts below.

Good	Bad

Lesson **7** **BEFORE READING**

Family Picnic Meal Plan

VOCABULARY

appetizer
food served before a meal

broccoli
a vegetable with green clusters of flowers eaten before they open

casserole
food baked and served in the same dish

celery
an herb with leaf stalks cooked or eaten raw

condiment
something used to flavor food

dessert
a sweet food served at the end of a meal

mustard
a condiment made from seeds of the mustard plant

pickle
preserved cucumbers

raisin
dried grapes

salad
vegetables (often lettuce) topped with a dressing

sausage
seasoned meat stuffed in a casing and cooked

Letters and Sounds

Write two words in each box below. If you are stumped, look through this book, talk to others, or use a dictionary.

b̸t	d̸g	l̸l
gh̸t	wh̸	p̸b
v̸h	f̸ at end of the word	

Use What You Know

Answer the questions below.

1. Does your family have picnics? Circle one.   Yes   No

2. If yes, who makes the food for the picnics? _____

   _____

3. Who usually makes the food for your family's special times?

   _____

   _____

Appetizers
Cherry tomatoes
Celery, raisins &
peanut butter
Cheese sticks

Side Dishes
Broccoli & rice salad
Green bean **casserole**
Corn on the cob
Potato **salad**
Bread and rolls
Baked beans

Meat Dishes
Baked ham
Sausage
Fried chicken

Family
Picnic
Meal Plan

Drinks
Lemonade
Iced tea
Water

Condiments
Pickles
Butter
Mustard
Salt

Desserts
Oatmeal cookies
Apple pie
Chocolate cake
Ice cream
sandwiches

Lesson **7** **AFTER READING** Family Picnic Meal Plan

STRATEGY

Reread or Read Ahead is a reading strategy. Use these strategies to look over a reading piece before you decide which parts interest you.

LIFE SKILLS

Information maps present information as small, connected units. Information maps help you find information quickly and easily.

CRITICAL THINKING

You may want to sort information when you read. For example, think about which foods you like and do not like in the meal plan on page 39. Doing this helps you pay attention when you read.

Reading Comprehension

Read the family picnic meal plan on page 39. Then answer the questions below.

1. **Reread or Read Ahead:** Write two food items you would like to make.

   _____

   _____

2. **Main Idea and Details:** The main idea is the most important idea in a paragraph, passage, or page. The main idea is supported by details. Circle the correct answer below about the main idea and details on page 39.

   A The meal plan does not have enough words to have main ideas and details.

   B The meal plan has only main ideas and details.

   C The meal plan has three main ideas.

3. **Fact or Opinion:** A **fact** is a statement that can be proved. An **opinion** is a statement of belief. It cannot be proved. Write one fact and one opinion about the meal plan.

   Fact _____

   _____

   Opinion_____

   _____

4. **Organize Ideas:** Write up to three food items from the meal plan that you like. Then write up to three food items you do not like.

Foods I Like	Foods I Do Not Like

When you plan a picnic, think about food safety. Spoiled food can make people sick.

To keep foods cool, pack an insulated cooler with ice or gel packs. Pack food right from the refrigerator or freezer into the cooler.

Food left out in the sun won't stay safe long. So, keep the cooler in the shade at the picnic. Keep the lid closed and don't open it often. Add more ice if it melts. Once gel packs and other cold sources melt, food is not safe—throw it away.

LANGUAGE

A **complex sentence** has an introductory phrase. Use a comma after the introductory phrase.

Examples:
- If Darrin comes soon, let's get ice cream.
- After school is done, Thu plans to find a job.

Letters and Sounds Review

Read the words in the box. Then write the words where they belong below.

doubt	while	cupboard	bright	ballet
wedge	night	ghost	ballet	depot

1. Has a **silent t** _____

2. Has a **silent h** _____

3. Has a **silent b** _____

4. Has a **silent h** _____

5. Has a **silent h** _____

6. Has a **silent gh** _____

7. Has a **silent d** _____

8. Has a **silent p** _____

9. Has a **silent h** _____

10. Has a **silent gh** _____

Language

Add the missing commas to the sentences below.

1. I need to stop at the store and buy chips pickles and cookies for the picnic.

2. When I stop for gas I'll buy cheese and bread.

3. After I heard the news I called Tammy.

4. When the music started we all jumped up to dance.

5. With this plan I think everything will work out OK.

6. After school Lora goes to her job.

7. Because he needed money Trent kept looking for a job.

8. If Donna and Andie both come we will need another chair.

9. After Edwardo started the grill Carmen opened the jar of pickles.

10. Because we all like mashed potatoes we are making a lot.

Replace This: Fill in the picnic meal plan below with foods you and your family like. Also, write some other things you would need on a picnic.

Family Picnic Meal Plan

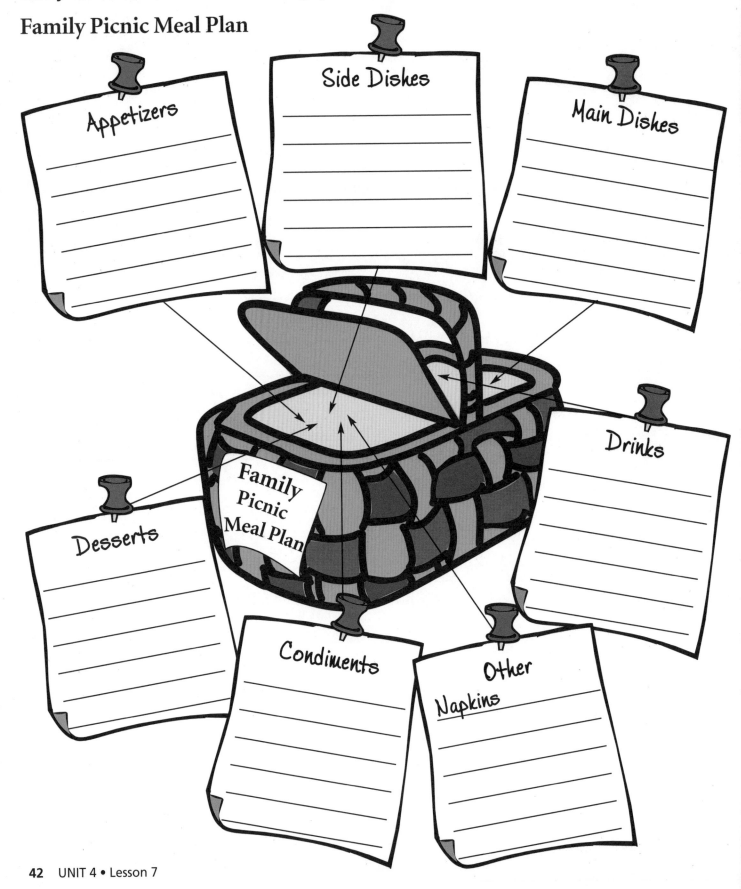

Your Own Information Map

WORD SKILLS

Below are three prefixes and their meanings.

de—opposite of
non—not
fore—before

Word Skills

Match a prefix from Box A with a base word from Box B. Write the new word where it belongs below.

A	de	B	ice	go	sense	code
	non		front	stop	brief	see
	fore		sight	fat	rail	bug

1. Can you _____ my computer?

2. The two-year-old ran _____ for 30 minutes.

3. _____ tells me that it is not a good idea.

4. Do you think _____ ice cream tastes good?

5. Let's bring it to the _____ and discuss it.

6. See if Dane can _____ the secret message.

7. It's too late. Let's _____ the last stop.

8. It all sounds like a bunch of _____ to me.

9. I hope the train does not _____ in the bad weather.

10. I didn't _____ this problem.

11. We had to wait for them to _____ the airplane.

12. We will _____ all of you before you leave.

Use What You Know

Find an information map in a magazine, newspaper, or book. Tape, staple, or glue the information map to page 44. Then answer the questions below.

1. Where did you find your information map? _____

2. Why do you think someone made this information map?

_____

Lesson

8 READING   Your Own Information Map

Look for an information map in a magazine, newspaper, or book. Make a copy of the information map. Tape, staple, or glue the information page to this page.

Lesson

8

AFTER READING

Your Own Information Map

CRITICAL THINKING
Information maps show relationships between ideas. Be sure the relationships still work if you change an information map.

Reading Comprehension

Read the information map on page 44. Then answer the questions below.

1. **Reread or Read Ahead:** Write three interesting details about your information map below.

   _____

   _____

   _____

2. **Main Idea and Details:** Fill in the blanks below.

   Main Idea The information map on page 44 is mostly about

   _____

   Details Write two details about a main idea in your information map.

   _____

   _____

   _____

3. **Fact or Opinion:** Write one fact and one opinion using information from your information map.

   Fact _____

   _____

   Opinion _____

   _____

4. **Replace this:** On your own paper, make an information map about something you like to do.

Language Review

On your own paper, write four sentences about picnics that use the items below.

- one compound sentence
- one sentence with a comma between two adjectives that tell about the same noun
- two sentences with a comma after an introductory phrase

When you write your sentences, do not add the punctuation. Then trade with a classmate. Add punctuation to each other's sentences.

WRITING
When writing facts, be exact. Information that is incomplete or wrong can be confusing.

Writing

Write one or two paragraphs about the information on page 44 below. Use more paper if needed. Include facts from the information map. Use the facts correctly.

When you are done, proofread your story. Make any changes. Then trade with a classmate and proofread each other's paragraphs. Get your paragraphs back. Make any changes. Write your final paragraphs.

_____

_____

_____

_____

_____

_____

_____

_____

_____

_____

_____

_____

Career Connection

Brainstorm ten jobs connected with the foods on page 39. Write the jobs below.

1. Jobs Connected with the Foods on the Family Picnic Meal Plan

A _____

B _____

C _____

D _____

E _____

F _____

G _____

H _____

I _____

J _____

2. Look at your list of jobs above. What two jobs interest you?

_____

_____

3. How can you find more information about these jobs?

_____

_____

Lesson **9** **BEFORE READING**

Measurement and Size Matches

VOCABULARY

bust
the part of the body between the neck and the waist; the chest

chart
information given in rows and columns

female
a woman or girl

hip
the meeting of the pelvis and the femur bone, between the waist and the thigh

male
a man or boy

measurement
finding the size

standard
according to rule

waist
the part that circles the narrow area between the ribs and the pelvis

Letters and Sounds

Circle the correct word to complete the sentences below.

1. The bear (cub, cube) played with its mother.

2. After her bath, Tenny wrapped in a fluffy orange (rob, robe).

3. Ryan wore a monkey (costume, costly) to the party.

4. I made a (mistake, mistook) on the first page of my homework.

5. I usually (hid, hide) the gifts under the bed. This time, I (hid, hide) them in the car.

6. I (hate, hat) that bright green (hate, hat).

7. I'm going to sleep when I (company, complete) this story.

8. (Pet, Pete) wrote a story about a teen who had too many shirts.

9. Please sit (beside, belittle) me on this bench.

Use What You Know

Answer the questions below.

1. Clothing sizes vary from brand to brand. Why is this true?

_____

_____

2. Sergio has two shirts. The clothing label for the first shirt says medium. The clothing label for the second shirt says size 38, neck 15. Which clothing label gives the most information?

_____

Why? _____

_____

READING Measurement and Size Matches

Teen Clothing Size Charts

Male Size Chart, in inches

Size	Chest	Waist	Neck
XS	30–33	24–27	13–13.5
S	34–36	28–30	14–14.5
M	37–40	31–34	15–15.5
L	41–44	35–39	16–16.5
XL	45–48	40–44	17–17.5
XXL	49–52	45–48	18–18.5
XXXL	53–56	49–52	19–19.5

Female Size Chart, in inches

Size	Size	Bust	Waist	Hips 1*	Hips 2**
XS	2–4	28–32	24–26	30–34	34–35
S	6–8	30–35	26–28	35–38	36–38
M	10–12	33–38	28–31	39–41	39–41
L	14–16	36–42	31–35	42–44	42–44
XL	18–20	40–46	35–38	45–48	45–48
XXL	22–24	44–51	38–45	49–54	49–54
XXXL	26–28	50–57	45–50	55–60	55–60

* Measure half way between waist and fullest part of hips.
** Measure at fullest part of hips (**standard** hip **measurement**)

Measurement and Size Matches

Reading Comprehension

Read the size charts on page 49. Then answer the questions below.

1. **Organize Ideas:** Write the best sizes for each person.

	Johan Chest: 42″ Waist: 34″ Neck: 16″	Nancy Bust: 34″ Waist: 27″ Hips: 39″
Shirt		
Pants		

2. **Think Further:** Where would a girl with a 20 inch waist and 26 inch hips find clothes that fit?

   _____

3. **Alike and Different:** Clothing sizes are not the same between males and females. Look at male medium and female medium. Write one thing that is alike and one thing that is different.

   _____

   _____

4. **Cause and Effect:** Answer the **What If** questions below.

Jeff has a 38 inch waist. **What if** he buys size Large pants?	➜	A

Moira has 41 inch hips and a 31 inch waist. **What if** her hips and waist grow by an inch?	➜	B

Holly has a 39 inch waist. **What if** she buys a size S shirt?	➜	C

Letters and Sounds Review

Circle the words below that follow the CVCe rule. For words with two or more syllables, look at the last syllable to see if it follows the CVCe rule.

1. give	11. bite	21. place
2. inside	12. none	22. broke
3. size	13. lake	23. home
4. amuse	14. rope	24. airplane
5. twice	15. joke	25. come
6. plane	16. costume	26. surprise
7. love	17. excuse	27. someone
8. make	18. necklace	28. bone
9. these	19. awake	29. whale
10. nose	20. beside	30. imagine

LANGUAGE

Use a comma after an introductory **yes** or **no**. Below are two examples.

- Yes, my middle name is Orville.
- No, I haven't eaten lunch yet.

Language

Add the missing commas to the sentences below. Two sentences will not need a comma.

1. No I'm not going to the football game.

2. Yes I got here fast because the bus was early.

3. Yes the radio is on.

4. No it's not cold enough for a winter coat.

5. Shirin wrote "yes" for number ten.

6. Yes Todd bought a new belt.

7. Are you Thad? No that's my brother. I'm Leon.

8. I have no idea.

Some clothes have **general sizes** such as Small (S), Medium (M), Large (L), and Extra Large (XL). A size Small can fit someone who wears a size 6 or 8.

Other clothes have **number sizes** such as 6, 12, $15\frac{1}{2}$, or 20.

General sizes and number sizes are different for men, women, children, and teens.

You may need to try on two or more sizes to find clothing that fits. Sometimes two sizes will fit you, depending on the style and clothing brand.

Life Skills Focus

Read the Life Skills box to the left. Then fill in the chart below with your sizes. If you do not know your sizes, check your clothing or ask a family member or friend. You can also go to a store and try on clothing. If you wear more than one size such as M and L, write both sizes in the chart.

Items	General Sizes	Number Sizes
Socks		
Belt		
Jeans		
Shirt or blouse		
T-shirt		
Sweat shirt		
Jacket		
Gloves		
Shoes		

Your Own Size Chart

WORD SKILLS

Below are three suffixes and their meanings.

less—without
ness—state or degree
ment—action

Word Skills

Add the suffix less, ness, or ment to each word below. Write the new word on the line. If needed, check a dictionary for spelling. Draw a picture of each new word below.

1. excite, _____

4. spot, _____

2. happy, _____

5. move, _____

3. sleep, _____

6. close, _____

Use What You Know

Find a clothing size chart. You can find them attached to clothing, in a magazine or mail order catalog, or on the Internet. Tape, staple, or glue the clothing size chart or a copy to page 54. Then answer the questions below.

1. Where did you find your size chart? _____

2. Do you think the sizes on this chart are the same as the sizes you usually wear? Circle one.   Yes   No

Find a clothing size chart. You can find them attached to clothing, in a magazine or mail order catalog, or on the Internet. Tape, staple, or glue the clothing size chart or a copy to this page.

Your Own Size Chart

Reading Comprehension

Read the size chart on page 54. Then answer the questions below.

1. **Organize Ideas:** Fill in the best sizes for each person.

	Johan Chest: 42" Waist: 34" Hips: 41" Neck: 16"	Nancy Bust: 34" Waist: 27" Hips: 39"
Shirt		
Pants		
Belt		

2. **Read for Details:** Which of the following people can use the charts?

   _____ Teen males   _____ Teen females   _____ Adult women

   _____ Adult men   _____ Children

3. **Cause and Effect:** Answer the two **What If** questions below.

What if you bought a shirt using the size chart and the shirt was too small?	➤	
What if you guess at your body measurements and you are wrong?	➤	

4. **Alike and Different:** Write one way that the size charts on pages 49 and 54 are alike.

   _____

   Write one way that the size charts on pages 49 and 54 are different.

   _____

Language Review

On your own paper, write five sentences about clothing that use the items below.

- one compound sentence
- one sentence with a comma between two adjectives that tell about the same noun
- one sentence with a comma after an introductory phrase
- two sentences with a comma after an introductory yes or no

When you write your sentences, do not add the punctuation. Then trade with a classmate. Add punctuation to each other's sentences.

Writing

WRITING
Write in a journal about what you are learning. This can help you better understand what you learn.

Start a journal about learning to read better. To begin, look through pages 8 to 56. Read the boxes on the pages. Choose two or more helpful tips and write them in your journal. Then write why they are helpful. When finished, proofread your work. Make any changes.

Career Connection

Many people work in the clothing business. Below are ten jobs that have to do with clothing. Put a check ✔ in the box if you think you may or may not like each job.

Jobs	I may like	I may not like
1. Cleaning Person: Cleans the store		
2. Photographer: Photographs models and clothing		
3. Clothing Designer: Creates new clothing designs		
4. Salesperson: Helps customers		
5. Fabric Designer: Creates new fabric prints		
6. Model: Wears new clothes in shows and for photos		
7. Ad Person: Plans ways to advertise clothing		
8. Factory Worker: Runs machines that make fabric		
9. Garment Worker: Sews clothing		
10. Truck Driver: Brings clothing around the country		

11. What job do you think you would like the most?

_____

Why? _____

_____

April Charges

PHONICS

Long a can be spelled in many ways.

Examples:

CVCe	lake
a	acorn
ai	rain
ay	play
ea	great
ei	vein
ey	they

VOCABULARY

agreement
a written or spoken contract between people or companies

charge
cost; price

current
now; in the present time

cycle
series of events that happen over and over

invoice
a bill to be paid

online
on the Internet

service
work done for others as part of a job

total amount due
total money to be paid for services

Letters and Sounds

Fill in the blanks below with letters to make correctly spelled long a words. Use the box to help check for words. Use a dictionary to check spelling.

a	m	w	pr	sn
b	n	fl	tr	sw
d	s	br	str	sh
l	t	gr	st	th

1. _____ ain

2. _____ ain

9. _____ eigh

10. _____ eigh

17. _____ ane

18. _____ ane

3. _____ ake

4. _____ ake

11. _____ ate

12. _____ ate

19. _____ ait

20. _____ ait

5. _____ ay

6. _____ ay

13. _____ ey

14. _____ ey

21. _____ ape

22. _____ ape

7. _____ eak

8. _____ eak

15. _____ ail

16. _____ ail

23. _____ ble

24. _____ ces

Use What You Know

1. The telephone is an important part of life. About how much time do you spend talking on the telephone each day?_____

2. How many telephones are in your home? _____

Cell King

Gail Sheigh
342 East Grey Way
Bayside, Maine 04915

Customer
someone
who pays
for a product
or service

Here's how to reach us:
• www.cellking.com
• 1-888-555-6543
• 234 from your wireless phone

Date of Invoice: 04/13/05
Due Date: 04/25/05

Summary of Monthly Charges for **Customer** Number 4352345
Wireless Number, Multi-Line Account **Agreement**

Starting Balance	Payments Received	Late Payment Charge	Current Monthly Charges
323.73	323.73 credit	.00	226.46

Credit
money in a
person's favor in
an account

Your billing **cycle** began on 03/12/05 and ended on 04/11/05

Current Monthly Charges
(207) 555-1234 Tess Sheigh   35.82
(207) 555-1235 Paul Sheigh   94.38
(207) 555-1236 Kolbe Sheigh   39.94
(207) 555-1237 Gail Sheigh   56.32

Total Monthly Charges   226.46
Total Amount Due   **226.46** **Billed to Charge Card****

Total Amount Due
226.46

You can pay your invoice **online** on the Internet at www.cellking.com
CELL KING THANKS YOU FOR YOUR BUSINESS

• •

Please return this part with your payment

Questions?
• www.cellking.com
• 1-888-555-6543 and ask
  for Customer **Service**

Payment
to give
money for

THIS IS NOT A BILL—DO NOT PAY
Customer Name: Gail Sheigh

Send **payment** to:
Cell King
P.O. Box 4326
Hampton, Virginia 23300

Due Date: 04/25/05
Amount Due: $226.46
Amount Paid: $_____

11 AFTER READING April Charges

Cell, or **wireless,** telephones are portable. You can carry a cell phone anywhere.

A **multi-line** phone has two or more phone numbers. All the phone numbers ring in on the separate phone lines, but they can be answered on the same phone.

READING COMPREHENSION

You make connections when you tie related information together. When you make connections, you will better understand what you read.

LIFE SKILLS

Telephones customers receive a bill every month. The bill shows basic telephone services. The bill also shows any extra features such as call waiting and long distance calls.

Reading Comprehension

Read the telephone bill on page 59. Answer the questions below.

1. **Create a Picture:** Make a bar graph of the four telephone line charges. Write a title. Write labels for the horizontal and vertical lines. For help with your bar graph, see pages 9 or 12.

   Title: _____

   _____

   _____

   _____

   _____

   _____

   _____

2. **Make Connections:** Why are the words "DO NOT PAY" on the bill?

   _____

   _____

3. **Replace This:** The charges on the bill are listed under four headings. Rewrite each heading with different words, but keep the same meaning of the heading.

A	B	C	D
323.73	323.73 credit	.00	226.46

READING COMPREHENSION

Reading skills are often studied one at a time. However, you can use two or more together. For example, when you look at the parts of a reading passage, you can then understand the whole.

4. Look at the Pieces and Understand: Read the two lines in the shaded area near the top of the bill. The two lines are broken into parts in the chart below. Tell the meaning of each part in your own words.

Part of Bill	What It Means
Summary of	**A**
Monthly Charges	**B**
for Account 4352345	**C**
Wireless Number	**D**
Multi-Line Account	**E**

Letters and Sounds Review

Read the clues below. All the words in the puzzle use long a. Write each word in the puzzle.

Clues

1. Very good
2. A vehicle that runs on tracks
3. Noise a horse makes
4. Sleet
5. Not able to walk properly
6. To get free, to get out and away
7. An animal hunted or seized for food

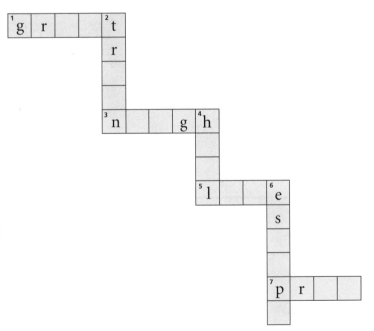

Add the missing commas to the sentences below.

Use a comma between spoken words and the rest of the sentence. Do not use a comma if a question mark or exclamation point is used. Below are four examples.

■ Dawn said, "Let's go on Tuesday."

■ "Let's go soon," Miguel said.

■ "No!" said Avi. "I'm not ready."

■ "What did you say?" Li asked.

1. Dane read his telephone bill. "I went over my minutes this month" he said.

2. Jenna said "Please be more careful."

3. Erin asked "Don't those extra minutes cost a lot?"

4. Inga said "I want a blue telephone."

5. "This telephone only comes in black purple or red" said the salesperson.

6. Inga pointed to the red telephone and said "I'll take that one."

7. The salesperson shouted "Hurrah! I sold my first cell phone."

Life Skills Focus

Many bills have a Change of Address area. This area is where you write your new address after you have moved. Below is a change of address form. Fill in the form. Use your current home address and telephone number for this form.

LIFE SKILLS

Keep your bills coming after you move. To do this, change your address with companies that send you bills.

You are responsible for your bills. You must pay them. This is true even if you don't get your bills in the mail.

If you don't pay your bills, you could lose services or get a bad credit rating.

Cell King

Change of Address

Please print clearly. Call 1-888-555-6543 with questions.

Your Name _____

New Address _____

City_____ State _____ Zip _____

Home Phone _____

Lesson

12

BEFORE READING

Your Own Telephone Bill

WORD SKILLS

The suffix **ure** turns verbs into nouns. Below are four patterns to add the suffix **ure**.

depart + ure = departure

❖ ❖ ❖

proceed − ed + d + ure = procedure

❖ ❖ ❖

treat − t + s + ure = treasure

❖ ❖ ❖

sign + at + ure = signature

Word Skills

Add the suffix ure to the words below. Use a dictionary to check spellings. Write the new words where they belong below. On your own paper, write a sentence using each new word.

1. expose _____   **5.** press _____

2. furnish _____   **6.** please _____

3. fail _____   **7.** close _____

4. mix _____

Use What You Know

Find a telephone bill page that shows the cost of services. Cover any personal information. Make a copy. Tape, staple, or glue the copy to page 64. Then answer the questions below.

1. How many pages were in the whole telephone bill? _____

2. Why is a telephone bill longer than one page?

_____

_____

_____

3. Why should you always check your telephone bill each month?

_____

_____

_____

READING   Your Own Telephone Bill

Find a telephone bill page that shows costs of services. Cover any personal information. Make a copy. Tape, staple, or glue the copy to this page.

Your Own Telephone Bill

Reading Comprehension

Read the telephone bill on page 64. Then answer the questions below.

1. **Create a Picture:** On your own paper, make a bar graph of four telephone charges. Write a title for the bar graph. Write labels for the horizontal and vertical lines. For help with a bar graph, see pages 9 or 12.

2. **Make Connections:** Put a star on the map below to show where you live. Then put a square on the map to show where to mail telephone payments.

3. **Look at the Pieces:** What is the first date of service on the bill?

   _____

   What is the last date of service on the bill? _____

4. **Understand:** Does the bill include telephone services other than basic service? Circle one.   Yes   No   If yes, tell about them below.

   _____

   _____

To sum up, write the overall idea in a few words or sentences. You can sum up many things you read.

Language Review

On your own paper, write five sentences that use the items below.

- one compound sentence
- one sentence where a comma between two adjectives that tell about the same noun
- one sentence with a comma after an introductory phrase
- one sentence with a comma after an introductory yes or no
- one sentence with a comma to separate spoken words from the rest of the sentence

When you write your sentences, do not add punctuation. Then trade with a classmate. Add punctuation to each other's sentences.

Writing

Why do you use a telephone? Write a paragraph below that sums up three or more reasons. When you are finished, read what you have written. Make sure it says what you mean. Then proofread and make any changes.

_____

_____

_____

_____

_____

_____

_____

_____

_____

_____

_____

_____

_____

CAREER

Letter names can be hard to understand over the telephone. Operators use words and names to make sure the letters are understood. To spell Kai, they may say, "K as kite, a as in apple, and i as in it."

The United States military and many other places use the code below.

A	Alfa
B	Bravo
C	Charlie
D	Delta
E	Echo
F	Foxtrot
G	Golf
H	Hotel
I	India
J	Juliett
K	Kilo
L	Lima
M	Mike
N	November
O	Oscar
P	Papa
Q	Quebec
R	Romeo
S	Sierra
T	Tango
U	Uniform
V	Victor
W	Whiskey
X	X-ray
Y	Yankee
Z	Zulu

Career Connection

Read the Career box on the left. Then read the example below to understand how to use the military code list. Write the letters of your first and last name below. Leave a space between your first and last name. Then write your name using the military code to make sure the letters are understood.

Example: Using the Military Code for Mike Thom

Letters	Code Words
M	Mike
I	India
K	Kilo
E	Echo
T	Tango
H	Hotel
O	Oscar
M	Mike

Your First and Last Name

Letters	Code Words

Lesson **13** **BEFORE READING**

Electricity Bill

VOCABULARY

detach
to remove

electricity
electric current used as a source of power

energy
usable power

local
referring to a smaller area such as a city, town, or district

natural gas
gas that comes from the earth's crust

payable
able to be paid in different ways

portion
a part or section

Letters and Sounds

Fill in the blanks below with letters that form correctly spelled long e words. Use the box to help you check for words. Use a dictionary to check spelling.

b	n	fl	gr
d	p	gl	spr
f	r	pl	sp
h	s	fr	sw
m	t		

1. _____ ea

2. _____ ea

7. _____ eed

8. _____ eed

13. _____ ieve

14. _____ elieve

3. _____ eet

4. _____ eet

9. _____ ee

10. _____ ee

15. _____ iece

16. _____ iece

5. _____ e

6. _____ e

11. _____ eceive

12. _____ eceive

17. _____ onkey

18. _____ onkey

Use What You Know

Answer the questions below.

1. Are electricity and gas on one bill in your area? Circle one.   Yes   No

2. What are the names of the electric and gas companies in your area?

_____

_____

QUESTIONS? WRITE LOGAN COUNTY ELECTRICITY AND NATURAL GAS, P.O. BOX 46433, PRATT, KANSAS 67124 OR CALL CUSTOMER SERVICE (316) 555-2311 OR VISIT US ONLINE AT www.loganelect.com

Logan County Electricity

Andrew T. Chung
45 West Albert Street
Pratt, Kansas 67124

Billing Date: 11/26
Customer Number:
11453-34-3453

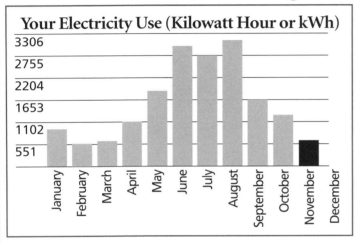

Your Electricity Use (Kilowatt Hour or kWh)

	Current Month	Previous Month	Last Year
Days on Bill	30	32	31
kWh Used	829	1,467	845
Average kWh Each Day	27.6	52.4	27.3
Cost Each Day	$1.97	$3.49	$1.72

Balance Due

On or before December 12, pay:	$72.32
After December 12, pay:	$77.32
Previous Bill 10/25/05	$120.53
Payments THANK YOU	− $120.53
Balance	$0.00
Electricity Charge	$59.15
Local Services	$12.21
State and Local Sales Tax	$0.96
Total **Energy** Balance	$72.32

• •

Please **detach** and mail with payment. If paying in person, please give both **portions**.

Customer: Andrew T. Chung
45 West Albert Street
Pratt, Kansas 67124

Please pay this amount on or before December 12: **$72.32**
Please pay this amount after December 12: $77.32
Customer Number: 11453-34-3453

Send payment to: Logan County Electricity and **Natural Gas,** P.O. Box 46433, Pratt, Kansas 67124
OR Make payment in person at any local Food Cart Store.
Make check **payable** to Logan Country Electricity.

Electricity Bill

Reading Comprehension

Read the electric bill on page 69. Then answer the questions below.

1. **Use Context Clues:** Choose one word from the bill that you do not know. Write the unknown word below. Complete the context clue box. Then write what the unknown word means.

   Unknown Word _____

   Helpful words in the same sentence or phrase _____

   Helpful sentence or phrase before or after the word _____

   _____

   Other _____

   What the Word Means _____

2. **Solve This:** Look at the high and low months on the bar graph. What does this pattern show?

   _____

   _____

3. **Group Ideas:** Put a check ✔ beside each category Andrew T. Chung belongs to.

   A _____ People who are using more electricity this year than last

   B _____ People who paid their electric bills on time last month

   C _____ People who pay their electric bills with automatic withdrawal

4. **Picture It and Make a Picture:** Look at the bar graph on the bill. Think of one way you could show this same information in a different graph. Use your own paper to create the new graph.

Letters and Sounds Review

Read the words below. Circle all the long a words. Put a box around all the long e words. For words with two syllables, look at the last syllable to see if it is a long a or long e word.

1. sea	**11.** hey	**21.** said
2. late	**12.** funny	**22.** me
3. clay	**13.** hay	**23.** hem
4. sandy	**14.** steak	**24.** sweet
5. steam	**15.** last	**25.** head
6. plan	**16.** reign	**26.** relieve
7. plane	**17.** deceive	**27.** again
8. tail	**18.** money	**28.** she
9. sell	**19.** lied	**29.** honey
10. veil	**20.** my	**30.** peek

Language

Circle the correct verbs to make these sentences sound right.

1. Lance often (mail, mails) his bills late.

2. Mari (pay, pays) her bills on time.

3. They both (want, wants) to get a car.

4. The people at the bank (say, says) Mari will have no problem getting a car loan. After Mari (sign, signs) some papers, she can get loan money for her car.

5. Lance (feel, feels) sad because he can not get a car loan.

6. He (plan, plans) to start paying his bills on time.

7. When Lance (go, goes) to the bank in a year, he (hope, hopes) to get a car loan.

8. Lance (think, thinks) the bank people will give him a loan then.

9. Lance now (tell, tells) everyone to (pay, pays) bills on time.

10. Even if you don't (need, needs) a car loan, you want others to know you can handle your bills.

LANGUAGE

A verb must agree in number with its subject.

Add **s** or **es** to the verb when the subject is a **singular noun**.

■ The puppy wants a treat.
■ Juan wants to play the tuba.

Use the plural verb form when the subject is a **plural noun**.

■ Doi and Teri like to ski.
■ The twins are ready to leave.

Sometimes you can hear if the subject and verb disagree. Read the sentences aloud, quietly.

Do not agree:
■ The dogs is here.
■ The dog walk with me in the morning.

Agree:
■ The dogs are here.
■ The dog walks with me in the morning.

LIFE SKILLS

If you pay your bills on time, you do not pay a penalty, or extra cost. The penalty saved on one bill may be small. However, penalties add up over time.

Life Skills Focus

Read the Life Skills box on the left. If Andrew T. Chung pays his electricity bill late, he will pay a penalty. Complete the chart below to see how this penalty can add up over time.

1. How much is the penalty if one payment is late? $ ______ × 1 = $ ______

2. How much is the total penalty if 6 payments are late? $ ______ × 6 = $ ______

3. How much is the total penalty if one year of payments are late? $ ______ × 12 = $ ______

4. What could you buy with the money in Item 3?

____

____

5. How much is the total penalty if five years of payments are late? $ ______ × 60 = $ ______

6. What could you buy with the money in Item 5?

____

____

7. Why do you think companies add a penalty to late bills?

____

____

Your Own Utility Bill

Word Skills

Match a word from Box A with a prefix or suffix in Box B. Write the new word below. You can use more than one prefix or suffix for each word.

A					B	
mix	face	base	amaze		de	ness
part	shape	govern	kind		fore	ment
fail	eager	move	sleep		non	ure
close	happy	press	sense		less	
front	state	text	tour			

1. _____   8. _____   15. _____

2. _____   9. _____   16. _____

3. _____   10. _____   17. _____

4. _____   11. _____   18. _____

5. _____   12. _____   19. _____

6. _____   13. _____   20. _____

7. _____   14. _____

Use What You Know

Find one page from a utility bill. Cover any personal information and make a copy of the utility bill. Tape, staple, or glue the copy to page 74. Then answer the question below.

1. What are two questions you could ask about a utility bill? Write the questions below.

Question 1 _____

_____

Question 2 _____

_____

14 READING   Your Own Utility Bill

Find one page from a utility bill. Cover any personal information and make a copy of the utility bill. Tape, staple, or glue the copy to this page.

Lesson **14** **AFTER READING**   ## Your Own Utility Bill

READING COMPREHENSION

Use information in a reading piece along with your own ideas to get new information.

Reading Comprehension

Read the utility bill on page 74. Then answer the questions below.

1. **Use Context Clues:** Choose one word from the bill that you do not know. Write the unknown word below. Complete each context clue box. Then write what the unknown word means.

   Word I do not know _____

   Helpful words in the same sentence or phrase _____

   Helpful sentence or phrase before the word _____

   Helpful sentence or phrase after the word _____

   What does the word mean? _____

   _____

   _____

2. **Solve This:** Write one thing about the weather and the bill or about the person the bill belongs to.

   _____

   _____

3. **Group Ideas:** Look at the category statements in Item 3 on page 70. Then write a category statement that is true about the bill on page 74.

   _____

   _____

   _____

LIFE SKILLS

Many people who work in utility companies have cubicles or cubes. These work spaces often measure eight feet by eight feet. Tall dividers stand between each cube. Many cubes have a desk, chair, computer, and other tools.

4. **Picture It and Make a Picture:** Read the Life Skills box to the left. Then think of what a cubicle looks like. On your own paper, draw a picture of a cubicle office.

Language Review

Read the words below. Then use the words to write sentences about utility bills. Be sure the subjects and verbs agree.

1. (like) _____

_____

2. (likes) _____

_____

3. (smile) _____

_____

4. (smiles) _____

_____

5. (walk) _____

_____

6. (walks) _____

_____

WRITING

Read all the parts on a bill, even the small print. There's a lot of information packed into most bills.

Writing

Sum It Up: What are three important pieces of information on the utility bill on page 74? Write a summary below.

_____

_____

_____

_____

_____

_____

_____

CAREER

Customer service staff help customers who have questions or problems.

Customers are the current and future users of a company's products and services.

Career Connection

Read the Career box on the left. Then think of two problems or questions that someone may have about their utilities. This person would call the utility company's customer service. Write the two problems or questions below. Then write what you think the customer service staff would say.

Problem 1

Answer 1

Problem 2

Answer 2

Lesson *15* **BEFORE READING**

Job Application

Letters and Sounds

Fill in the blanks below with letters that form long i words. Use the box to help you check for words. Use a dictionary to check your spelling.

b d h i	l m p r	t fl sl br	cr pr str sm	sp sh

1. _____ ike

2. _____ ike

3. _____ y

4. _____ y

5. _____ ie

6. _____ ie

7. _____ ight

8. _____ ight

9. _____ ime

10. _____ ime

11. _____ ide

12. _____ ide

13. _____ ye

14. _____ ye

15. _____ i

16. _____ tem

17. _____ ile

18. _____ ile

Use What You Know

Answer the questions below.

1. Have you ever filled out a job application? Circle one.   Yes   No

2. Did any questions surprise you? Circle one.   Yes   No

   If yes, write one or two of the questions.

   _____

   _____

   _____

APPLICATION FOR EMPLOYMENT

Date _____

YOUR FACTS

Name _____ Telephone _____
  (LAST)   (FIRST)   (MIDDLE INITIAL)

Address _____
      (#)   (STREET)   (CITY)   (STATE)   (ZIP CODE)

E-mail Address _____

EMPLOYMENT DESIRED

Date You   Salary
Can Start _____ Wanted _____

Position _____

SCHOOLS

High School and College	Years There	Degree	Best Subjects

WORK EXPERIENCE

Name and Address of Company	Date Started	Date Left	Position and Supervisor

Why would you make a good worker? Write two reasons below.

1. _____

2. _____

SPECIAL SKILLS

1. _____

2. _____

Sign Your Name Here _____

Job Application

A **job application** is a standard form used to apply for a job. It provides information about your education and work experience.

LIFE SKILLS

Look your best when you fill out a job application at a company.

CRITICAL THINKING

You can often plan ahead when you picture something.

LIFE SKILLS

When filling out an application, read and follow directions. Give as much information as you can.

Reading Comprehension

Read the job application on page 79. Then answer the questions below.

1. **Main Ideas and Details:** The job application has some main ideas. Details support each main idea. One main idea and one detail has been filled in below. Write three more main ideas along with details.

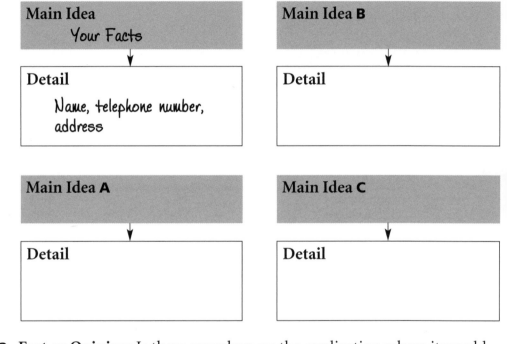

Main Idea
Your Facts

Detail
Name, telephone number, address

Main Idea **B**

Detail

Main Idea **A**

Detail

Main Idea **C**

Detail

2. **Fact or Opinion:** Is there any place on the application where it would be OK to write an opinion? Tell why or why not.

_____

_____

3. **Look at the Pieces:** Say you are at a company filling out the job application on page 79. What parts would you have trouble filling out quickly?

_____

_____

4. **Picture This:** Say you are at a company filling out a job application.

What would you be wearing? _____

_____

Letters and Sounds Review

Use the clues to complete the puzzle. All the words have a long a, e, or i.

Across
2. A bright _____ day
5. To say the words on a page
7. A horse's rope
8. To join the strings on a shoe
10. To tell how something works
12. A red vegetable
13. To write with a computer
15. Say good_____
17. An error

Down
1. A type of grain made into bread
2. Female of he
3. To make a stick into two pieces
4. A two-wheel vehicle
5. To understand clearly
6. A horse-like animal with long ears
8. him : he as them : _____
9. Not wrong
11. The fifth month
14. Having very white skin
16. Deep sadness

Language

Fill in the missing parts of this chart. One has been done for you.

Singular Subject	Singular Verb	Plural Subject	Plural Verb
I	see	We	sees
You	run	You	**1.** _____
He	eats	They	**2.** _____
I	know	We	**3.** _____
You	**4.** _____	You	**5.** _____
Cindra	**6.** _____	The Millers	**7.** _____
I	am	**8.** _____	**9.** _____
You	**10.** _____	**11.** _____	**12.** _____
Ryan	**13.** _____	We	**14.** _____

Use your neatest
writing to fill in
a job application.

Life Skills Focus

Read the directions below for each form. Then fill in each form. Do your neatest work. When finished, put a star beside the one that you think looks the best.

1. Print with a regular ink pen to fill out this form.

Date _____

Last Name_____   First Name _____

Telephone Number _____   E-mail Address _____

Address _____

City _____   State_____Zip _____

2. Write with an ink pen to fill out this form.

Date _____

Last Name_____   First Name _____

Telephone Number_____   E-mail Address _____

Address _____

City _____   State_____ Zip _____

3. Print with a fine felt tip pen to fill out this form.

Date _____

Last Name_____   First Name _____

Telephone Number _____   E-mail Address _____

Address _____

City _____   State_____ Zip _____

4. Write with an fine felt tip pen to fill out this form.

Date _____

Last Name_____   First Name _____

Telephone Number_____   E-mail Address _____

Address _____

City _____   State_____ Zip _____

Your Own Form

WORD SKILLS

How many of the abbreviations in Word Skills have you used?

_____

Word Skills

In each set, read the abbreviations on the left. Then draw a line to match them with what they stand for on the right. If you need help, use a dictionary or ask others.

SET 1		SET 3	
1. A.M.	Mistress	**13.** M.D.	nurse
2. P.M.	facsimile	**14.** Dr.	Reverend
3. Mr.	morning	**15.** R.N.	doctor
4. Mrs.	Mister	**16.** Rev.	road
5. TV	television	**17.** Ave.	doctor
6. fax	afternoon	**18.** Rd.	avenue
SET 2		**SET 4**	
7. lb	number	**19.** Blvd.	Senior
8. min	please reply	**20.** St.	and
9. No. or #	inches	**21.** Jr.	boulevard
10. " or in.	feet	**22.** Sr.	about
11. ' or ft	minimum	**23.** & or +	Junior
12. R.S.V.P.	pound	**24.** approx.	street

LIFE SKILLS

Forms are all around you. Below are common forms:

- bank deposit slips
- catalog order forms
- credit card and insurance applications
- driver's license forms
- information forms at the doctor's or dentist's office
- job applications
- rental and lease agreements
- season ticket forms

Use What You Know

Read the Life Skills box to the left. Find a form. Cover any personal information. Make a copy. Tape, staple, or glue the copy to page 84. Answer the question below.

1. How are forms different from graphs or charts? _____

_____

_____

16 READING   Your Own Form

Find a form. Cover any personal information. Make a copy of the form. Tape, staple, or glue the copy to this page.

Lesson **16** **AFTER READING** Your Own Form

LIFE SKILLS

Many forms ask for the same basic types of information. This includes your name, address, telephone number, and other personal information.

LIFE SKILLS

You can fill out most forms if you read and follow the instructions.

Reading Comprehension

Read the form on page 84. Then answer the questions below.

1. **Main Ideas and Details:** Write a main idea from the form below. Then write two details about the main idea.

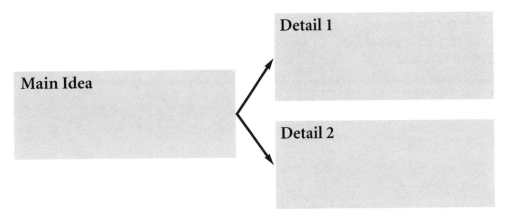

2. **Fact or Opinion:** Is there any place on the form where it would be OK to write an opinion? Circle one.   Yes   No

   Tell why or why not. _____

   _____

   _____

3. **Look at the Pieces:** Sometimes you do not want to write personal information on a form. Is there any information you do not want to write on this form? Circle one.   Yes   No

   Tell why or why not. _____

   _____

   _____

4. **Picture It:** Think about people who would fill out this form. Where do you see these people sitting as they fill out the form?

   _____

   _____

WRITING

Create a wallet or purse résumé and keep it with you. Use it to fill out job applications and other forms.

LIFE SKILLS

Many job applications ask for references. A reference is someone who can give information about your character or skills.

Writing

Complete the wallet or purse résumé below. Print small so your information will fit. Read over your work and make sure you have everything written down. Make a copy, fold it, and keep it in your wallet or purse.

Name _____

Address _____

Telephone Number _____

E-mail Address _____

EDUCATION

School_____Address _____

Degree/Subject _____Dates _____

School_____Address _____

Degree/Subject _____Dates _____

School Activities_____

EMPLOYMENT

Name of Employer _____

Address _____

Job Title _____Dates _____

Name of Employer _____

Address _____

Job Title _____Dates _____

Special Skills _____

REFERENCES

Name _____Title_____

Address _____

Telephone Number _____

Name _____Title_____

Address _____

Telephone Number _____

Name _____Title_____

Address _____

Telephone Number _____

Language Review

Use the words below in sentences about jobs. Be sure the subjects and verbs agree so that the sentences sound right.

1. (was) _____

_____

2. (were) _____

_____

3. (find) _____

_____

4. (finds) _____

_____

5. (drive) _____

_____

6. (drives) _____

_____

CAREER

All parts of a job application can make a difference. Be neat, complete, and correct when you fill out a form.

Career Connection

Look back on page 82 to find your neatest way to fill in a form. Use this way to complete the job application on page 79. Then fill in the form on page 84. Try not to make any mistakes. You can use your wallet or purse résumé from page 86 to complete the form.

Lesson 17 **BEFORE READING** Park Services

Long o can be spelled in many ways.

Examples:

CVCe	home
oe	toe
oa	boat
ow	snow
ou	shoulder
o	over

VOCABULARY

concession
a place selling
food or snacks

concrete
a mixture of cement, sand
or gravel, and water that
hardens as it dries

grill
item with parallel bars
to cook food over
a fire or charcoal

recreation
play, amusement, fun

shelter
something that covers or
protects from weather

snack
a small amount of food
eaten between meals

Letters and Sounds

Fill in the blanks below with letters to spell long o words. Use the ABC box to help you check for words. If you are not sure how to spell a word, use a dictionary.

b g h	j l n	o t v	z fl br	thr sp sh

1. _____ oke   9. _____ ote   17. _____ own

2. _____ oke   10. _____ ote   18. _____ own

3. _____ ow   11. _____ oulder   19. _____ ver

4. _____ ow   12. _____ oulder   20. _____ pen

                                        21. _____ dor

5. _____ oe   13. _____ old

6. _____ oe   14. _____ old

7. _____ oat   15. _____ one

8. _____ oat   16. _____ one

Use What You Know

1. Many cities in the United States have one or more parks. Many people

   think that the parks are important. Why? _____

   _____

2. What are three services that parks often provide? _____

   _____

   _____

READING Park Services

	Read Park	Krape Park	Oakdale Park
Recreation			
Pool	Two family, one child	None	One family
Ball Diamonds	3 T-ball 2 Full-size baseball 2 Softball	8 Full-size baseball 4 Softball	2 T-ball 10 Little League
Skateboard Course	1	0	0
Nature Trails	0	4	12
Concessions	3 Popcorn stands 2 Full **snack** stands	4 Full snack stands	3 Popcorn stands
Picnic Setups			
Picnic Tables	47 Wood 12 **Concrete**	32 Wood 45 Concrete	14 Wood 53 Concrete
Grills	12 Small 2 Large	14 Small 3 Large	21 Small
Shelter Houses	5 Open 2 With heat and air	3 Open	4 Open 3 With heat and air
Playgrounds			
Swings	15	7	19
Play Place	600 square feet	None	200 square feet
Slides	5 Straight 2 Curly	4 Straight 3 Curly	2 Straight 2 Curly
Play Building	Firehouse Barn House	House Cabin	Fort Barn

Park Services

Reading Comprehension

STRATEGY

Make It Clear is a reading strategy. **Understand** is a comprehension skill. The two work together because understanding helps make ideas clear.

READING COMPREHENSION

Categories, or groups, are often the same as the main ideas in a reading piece.

CRITICAL THINKING

Think about cause and effect when you read. This helps make what you read more useful.

READING COMPREHENSION

Information charts give information of all kinds. Information charts show facts easily and quickly and are used in many places.

Reading Comprehension

Read the Park Services information chart on page 89. Then answer the questions below.

1. **Make It Clear and Understand:** Simon wants to take his six-year-old sister swimming. Which parks are good choices? _____

_____

2. **Group Ideas:** Write two reasons to go to each park below.

Read Park	Krape Park	Oakdale Park
A _____	C _____	E _____
B _____	D _____	F _____

3. **Cause and Effect:** Complete the sentences below.

Cause		Effect
If you want to order a hamburger	*Then* →	
If	*Then* →	she will probably not play ball at Krape Park.

4. **Make It Clear:** Complete the sentence below.

The Play Place at Oakdale is smaller than the one at Read Park. I know this is true because

_____

_____

Letters and Sounds Review

Circle all the words with long vowel sounds. The long vowel sound can be in the first or second syllable.

1. open
2. again
3. knead
4. believe
5. conceive
6. monkey
7. she
8. cost
9. buggy
10. make

11. stain
12. cloud
13. ray
14. veil
15. prey
16. some
17. break
18. mile
19. lie
20. head

21. sight
22. shy
23. dye
24. poke
25. Joe
26. moat
27. blow
28. boulder
29. been
30. teen

LANGUAGE

The verbs in sentences express tense. The verb tense tells the time when an action takes place.

Use **present tense** when the action is happening now or if it usually happens. Examples:

- I like jam on my toast.
- The team practices every day.
- Jackson fishes in the river all summer.

Language

Circle the correct verbs to make these sentences present tense.

1. Liam (works, worked) at Read Park.

2. He (is, was) working today.

3. Liam (will think, thinks) he has a great job.

4. He (cleaned, cleans) the pool.

5. He (will cook, cooks) hotdogs.

6. On rainy days, he (scrubs, scrubbed) the pool locker room.

7. Sometimes, Loni (paints, will paint) the small playhouses.

8. He (moved, moves) broken picnic tables. Then Talia (fixes, fixed) them.

9. Steve (liked, likes) to use the riding lawn mowers.

10. Bonita (will mow, mows) most of the time.

To find out what services a park has, you can:

- go to the park
- call the park office
- read a park brochure
- read a park's Web site

Life Skills Focus

Trial and Error: Answer the questions below.

1. Write the names of local parks where you could do each activity below. Then read the Life Skills box on the left. Check to be sure the parks you chose have the services. Put an **X** beside each activity you checked.

Service	Park You Chose	Check to Make Sure
Use a shelter house		
Swim		
Hike		
Play softball		
Grill		
Skateboard		
Buy snacks		

2. What local parks have you visited? _____

_____

_____

3. What park would you like to go to?_____

Why? _____

_____

_____

Your Own Information Chart

Word Skills

In each set, read the abbreviations on the left. Draw a line to what they stand for on the right. If you need help use a dictionary or ask others.

SET 1	
1. mpg	self-addressed, stamped envelope
2. ¢	at
3. C.O.D.	cent, money
4. SASE	package
5. pkg	mileage
6. @	pay money

SET 2	
7. .com	in addition
8. ASAP	teen movie
9. ATM	Internet company
10. FYI	as soon as you can
11. PG13	cash machine
12. P.S.	for your information

SET 3	
13. TBA	this and that
14. w/o	being nice
15. TLC	tell later
16. w/	large; extra large
17. misc.	with
18. Lg; XL	without

SET 4	
19. qty	paid
20. ID	and so on
21. pd	information
22. info	dollar, money
23. $	quantity
24. etc.	card with photo on it

LIFE SKILLS

Look for information charts in newspapers, magazines, and books. They are also in department stores, on the Internet, and in airports.

Use What You Know

Read the Life Skills box to the left. Find an information chart. Tape, staple, or glue it to page 94. Then answer the questions below.

1. Where did you find your information chart? _____

2. Why do you think the information chart was made? _____

_____

3. Write two types of information charts your classmates used. _____

_____

READING   Your Own Information Chart

Find an information chart in books, magazines, newspapers, or on the Internet. Tape, staple, or glue the information chart to this page.

Lesson **18** **AFTER READING**

Your Own Information Chart

Reading Comprehension

Read the information chart on page 94. Then answer the questions below.

1. **Understand:** Circle a phrase or sentence that is hard to understand. Rewrite it in your own words below.

   _____

   _____

2. **Group Ideas:** Write three main groups of information from your information chart below.

3. **Cause and Effect:** Write two cause and effect sentences below.

Cause		**Effect**

4. **Make It Clear:** Fill in the blanks below.

   I think people will use this chart to _____

   _____

   I think this is true because _____

   _____

Language Review

Circle the present tense verb in each set below. Then, write a sentence that uses each present tense verb. Be sure the subjects and verbs agree.

1. (see, saw, will see) _____

_____

2. (stood, stand, will stand) _____

_____

3. (pointed, will point, point) _____

_____

4. (felt, feels, will feel) _____

_____

5. (blink, blinked, will blink) _____

_____

6. (followed, will follow, follows) _____

_____

7. (gone, go, will go) _____

_____

8. (has eaten, ate, eat) _____

_____

Writing

On your own paper, write a summary about a park or an outdoor activity you like. Write one or two paragraphs and use active voice. When finished, proofread your writing. Make any changes.

CAREER

Many park jobs are seasonal. They last just a few months, often during busy times. In most parks, the busiest times are the summer months. Kids are not in school and have more time to go to parks.

Answer the questions about park jobs below.

1. Below is a list of park jobs. Put a check ✔ beside each one you might like to do.

____ Mow grass   ____ Lead children's games

____ Paint benches   ____ Take tickets

____ Build picnic tables   ____ Clean grills

____ Sell snacks   ____ Fill bird feeders

____ Lifeguard   ____ Pick up litter

____ Referee   ____ Empty trash cans

____ Rake leaves   ____ Put up and take down signs

2. Do you think you would like to work in a park? Circle one.   Yes   No

3. Why or why not? _____

_____

_____

_____

BEFORE READING

Tax Tables

PHONICS

Long u can be spelled in many ways.

Examples:

CVCe	tube
eu	feud
ew	few
oo	toon
ou	soup
ui	bruise
u	unicorn
ue	clue

VOCABULARY

filing
sending completed tax forms to the IRS

household
a family or group of people living together

income
amount of money earned during a certain time

jointly
together

least
smallest amount

married
having a husband or wife

separately
individually

tax
money people pay to the government

Letters and Sounds

Fill in the blanks below with letters to spell long u words. Use the box to help you check for words. If you are not sure how to spell a word, use a dictionary.

b	f	m	bl	sl	fr
c	j	n	cl	br	gr
d	l	s	fl	cr	tr

1. ___ ute

2. ___ ute

3. ___ uit

4. ___ uit

5. ___ oot

6. ___ oot

7. ___ ue

8. ___ ue

9. ___ ew

10. ___ ew

11. ___ eutral

12. ___ euth

13. ___ oop

14. ___ oop

15. ___ oup

16. ___ oup

17. ___ uise

18. ___ uise

19. ___ ude

20. ___ ude

21. ___ ood

22. ___ ood

23. ___ ued

Use What You Know

Answer the questions below.

1. What are tax tables like the ones on page 99 used for? _____

   _____

2. Where can you get tax tables like the ones on page 99? _____

   _____

READING Tax Tables

This is line 41 on an Income Tax form. You find the number on this tax table, and then write it on the Income Tax form.

People who make $20,000, but less than $20,050 look here. This table tells them how much income tax to pay.

A total of six tax tables are on each federal tax table page.

If line 41 income that's taxed is		And you are			
At **least**	But less than	Single	**Married filing jointly**	Married filing separately	Head of household
		Your **Tax** is—			
20,000					
20,000	20,050	2,704	2,404	2,704	2,504
20,050	20,100	2,711	2,411	2,711	2,511
20,100	20,150	2,719	2,419	2,719	2,519
20,150	20,200	2,726	2,426	2,726	2,526
20,200	20,250	2,734	2,434	2,734	2,534
20,250	20,300	2,741	2,441	2,741	2,541
20,300	20,350	2,749	2,449	2,749	2,549
20,350	20,400	2,756	2,456	2,756	2,556
20,400	20,450	2,764	2,464	2,764	2,564
20,450	20,500	2,771	2,471	2,771	2,571
20,500	20,550	2,779	2,479	2,779	2,579
20,550	20,600	2,786	2,486	2,786	2,586
20,600	20,650	2,794	2,494	2,794	2,594
20,650	20,700	2,801	2,501	2,801	2,601
20,700	20,750	2,809	2,509	2,809	2,609
20,750	20,800	2,816	2,516	2,816	2,616
20,800	20,850	2,824	2,524	2,824	2,624
20,850	20,900	2,831	2,531	2,831	2,631
20,900	20,950	2,839	2,539	2,839	2,639
20,950	21,000	2,846	2,546	2,846	2,646
21,000					
21,000	21,050	2,854	2,554	2,854	2,654
21,050	21,100	2,861	2,561	2,861	2,661
21,100	21,150	2,869	2,569	2,869	2,669
21,150	21,200	2,876	2,576	2,876	2,676
21,200	21,250	2,884	2,584	2,884	2,684
21,250	21,300	2,891	2,591	2,891	2,691
21,300	21,350	2,899	2,599	2,899	2,699
21,350	21,400	2,906	2,606	2,906	2,706
21,400	21,450	2,914	2,614	2,914	2,714
21,450	21,500	2,921	2,621	2,921	2,721
21,500	21,550	2,929	2,639	2,929	2,729
21,550	21,600	2,936	2,686	2,936	2,736
21,600	21,650	2,944	2,644	2,944	2,744
21,650	21,700	2,951	2,651	2,951	2,751
21,700	21,750	2,959	2,659	2,959	2,759
21,750	21,800	2,966	2,666	2,966	2,766
21,800	21,850	2,974	2,674	2,974	2,774
21,850	21,900	2,981	2,681	2,981	2,781
21,900	21,950	2,989	2,689	2,989	2,789
21,950	22,000	2,996	2,696	2,996	2,796

These four columns give different tax amounts for people if they are:

- single
- married
- married and filling out tax forms alone
- single with children

People find their income amounts in these tables. People who make from $20,000 up to $21,999 use these two tax tables.

LIFE SKILLS

The federal government collects **taxes** from people who work. The amount of taxes is based on **income**, or how much money is earned in a year. Taxes are listed in tax tables. The amount of taxes changes, so the government prints new tax tables each year.

Tax Tables

Reading Comprehension

Read the tax tables on page 99. Then answer the questions below.

1. **Reread and Alike and Different:** Tell about the number pattern used for the numbers in the purple box.

   _____

   _____

   _____

2. **Solve This:** The tax table shows tax amounts for four groups of single and married people. Which group pays the least amount of tax?

   _____

   Which group pays the most amount of tax? _____

3. **Read for Details:** Write the tax amount for each of the people below.

   A Dale is married and earns $21,630. He and his wife are filing taxes together.   _____

   B Tara is single. She makes $20,400.   _____

   C Raja and Cass are married. Together they earn $21,926. They are filing a joint return.   _____

   D David is married, but he is filing his taxes separately. He earns $20,673.   _____

   E Binh is single. She earns $21,872.   _____

4. **Organize Ideas:** Why are the numbers 20,000 and 21,000 at the top of the boxes?

   _____

Letters and Sounds Review

Why didn't the tax man want to talk about his broken pencil? Use the clues to solve the puzzle. All the answers have long vowel sounds.

Clues

1. I don't know _____.
2. Rub out with a pencil end
3. The act of seeing, look
4. Worn over the body to protect clothes when cooking
5. Today I draw, yesterday I _____
6. Opposite of nephew
7. An outer winter clothing with long sleeves
8. To give money for goods
9. Used in the baking of bread
10. To think is true
11. Odd or silly
12. The part of the body between the ribs and hips

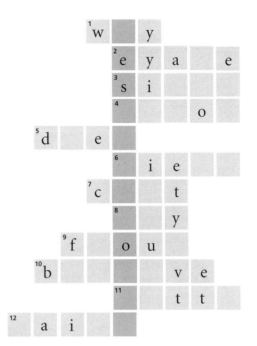

Verbs can express **past tense**. Use the past tense when the action has already happened.

Examples:

- I opened the mail.
- Jill swam in the lake last fall.
- Hod shut the car door.

Language

Circle the correct word to make each sentences past tense.

1. DeNorris (plans, planned) to pay his taxes.

2. He (writes, wrote) it on his calendar every day.

3. Leah (pays, paid) her taxes on April 12.

4. I (do, did) my taxes myself. I (used, will use) the tax tables.

5. Rico (paid, pays) a fine because he did not pay his taxes on time.

6. Cora (owes, owed) more money than last year.

7. I (bought, will buy) a television with the money I got back from my taxes.

8. Sami (did not, will not) get any money back.

9. I wonder if most people (got, get) money back.

10. It (took, takes) me about two hours to do my taxes.

W-2s are reports that companies must give to their workers and the government. W-2s tell the following information about you:

- your name and address
- your social security number
- the name and address of the place you worked
- the total money you made for one year
- the total money withheld from your checks for one year
- how much you paid in state taxes
- how much you paid in federal taxes

Life Skills Focus

By law, W-2s must be mailed out on or before January 31 each year. Some people get their W-2s in January. Other people get their W-2s by February 7. Federal taxes are due on or before April 15. Answer the questions below about taxes.

1. Use the current year and put the days in the four months below. Circle the February 7 and April 15 dates below.

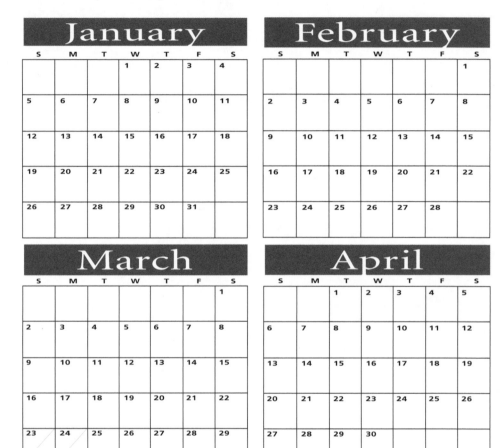

2. Say you get your W-2 on February 7. How many weeks do you have to do your taxes?

_____

3. The amount of taxes you pay depends on how much you earn. Why do you think people who make more money pay more taxes?

_____

_____

_____

Your Own Information Table

Word Skills

Write a homophone for each word below. On your own paper, write a sentence using one or both of the words.

1. dew, _____

2. see, _____

3. bear, _____

4. brake, _____

5. flour, _____

6. grate, _____

7. steal, _____

8. way, _____

9. made, _____

10. seen, _____

11. whether, _____

12. patience, _____

Use What You Know

Find an information table in books, magazines, newspapers, or on the Internet. Tape, staple, or glue the information table to page 104. Then answer the questions below.

1. How many columns are in your table? _____

2. Look at the tables your classmates put on page 104. What is the largest number of columns?_____ What is the smallest number of columns?_____

READING   Your Own Information Table

Find an information table in books, magazines, newspapers, or on the Internet. Tape, staple, or glue the information table to this page.

Your Own Information Table

Reading Comprehension

Read the information table on page 104. Then answer the questions.

1. **Alike and Different:** Write one way the information tables on pages 99 and 104 are alike. Then write one way they are different.

   Alike _____

   _____

   Different _____

   _____

2. **Solve This:** Do you think the information table on page 104 is useful? Circle one.   Yes   No   Why or why not? _____

   _____

   _____

3. **Read for Details:** Write three details from the information table below.

   A _____

   _____

   B _____

   _____

   C _____

   _____

4. **Organize Ideas:** Tell how the table is organized. _____

   _____

   _____

   _____

Language Review

Read the sentences below. Circle past or present to tell the tense of each of sentence.

1. Chad is 21 years old.   past   present

2. The snow stopped before midnight.   past   present

3. It was too late to make a plan.   past   present

Write sentences about paying taxes in the tenses below.

4. (present) _____

_____

5. (present) _____

_____

6. (past) _____

_____

THREE FRIENDS
Three friends share a house. They want to do their taxes, but lost their tax tables.
Denbe—Single, made $20,750
Ling—Married and filing separately, made $21,835
Elena—Single, made $21,305

Writing

Read the Three Friends box on the left. Find the taxes for Denbe, Ling, and Elena on page 99. Write an e-mail below to tell the three friends the tax numbers they each need. Proofread your e-mail and check your facts.

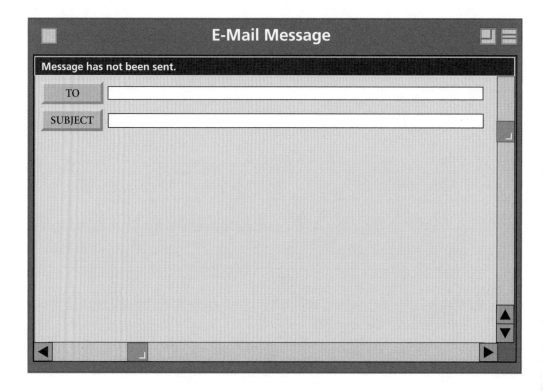

CAREER

Tax preparers work very hard in January, February, March, and April. They must be good at their work. Tax preparers also need to enjoy their work. If they didn't, they would have a hard time with the long hours and stress.

Read the Career box on the left. Then read the skills for a tax preparer below. Do you have any of these skills? Put a check ✔ beside each skill you think you have or do not have.

Tax Preparer Skills	Do Have	Do NOT Have
1. Is good at working with numbers		
2. Does not make mistakes very often		
3. Can handle stress		
4. Can work long hours for many days in a row		
5. Can work four months without taking a day off		
6. Can work with new ideas and numbers		
7. Can use an electronic calculator 10-key pad without looking		
8. Likes to work with computers		
9. Likes to work at a desk		
10. Enjoys working with the public		

11. Would you like to be a tax preparer? Circle one.   Yes   No

Why or why not? _____

_____

_____

BEFORE READING

Features of Toaster Models

PHONICS

A common long-vowel pattern is **v/cv,** or vowel-consonant-vowel with a syllable break after the first vowel.

Example: pa/per

Another common long-vowel pattern is **v/v,** or two vowels with a syllable break between them.

Example: cre/ate

VOCABULARY

bagel
ring-shaped roll of raised dough

brand
a name or trademark that identifies a company or its products

dial
a control knob

electronic
working by electricity

slice
a piece cut from a larger object

slot
a narrow opening

Letters and Sounds

Rewrite the words below into syllable, or parts, using the dotted lines. One has been done for you.

v / cv

begin _____be ǀ gin_____   **4.** later _____

1. broken _____   **5.** hotel _____

2. donut _____   **6.** student _____

3. final_____   **7.** open _____

v / v

8. duet_____   **12.** poem_____

9. neon _____   **13.** diet _____

10. react _____   **14.** science _____

11. lion _____   **15.** skier _____

Use What You Know

Answer the questions below.

1. Do you have a toaster at home? Circle one.   Yes   No

2. What are three things you want a toaster to do? _____

_____

_____

3. How much money would you pay for a toaster that does everything

you want it to do? _____

READING Features of Toaster Models

Toaster Buying Guide

Brand	Model	Space Saver	Two-Slice	Four-Slice	Extra-Wide Slots	Bagel Setting	Darkness Control	Quick Shut-Off	Cool-Touch Sides	Music Alarm	Cord Put-Away	Dust Cover	Fancy Sides	Modern Design	Dial Timer	Electronic Timer	Two Controls (4-slicers)	Under $25	$25–$50	$50–$100
Green Swan	GF2	✔	✔	–	–	–	✔	–	–	–	–	–	–	✔	✔	–	–	✔	–	–
Green Swan	GF3	✔	–	✔	–	–	✔	–	✔	–	–	–	✔	✔	–		✔	–	✔	–
Green Swan	GF4	–	–	✔	✔	✔	✔	✔	✔	–	✔	–	✔	✔	–	✔	✔	–	✔	–
Rowe Mead	Hero Toast	✔	–	✔	–	✔	✔	–	✔	–	–	–	–	✔	✔	–	✔	✔	–	–
Rowe Mead	Hero Toast Giant	✔	–	✔	✔	✔	✔	✔	✔	–	–	–	–	✔	–	✔	✔	–	–	✔
Blue Key	Kitchen Lady	–	–	✔	–	–	✔	–	–	–	–	–	–	✔	✔	–	–	✔	–	–
Blue Key	Kitchen Princess	✔	✔	–	–	✔	✔	–	✔	–	–	–	–	✔	✔	–	–	–	✔	–
Blue Key	Kitchen Queen	✔	–	✔	✔	✔	✔	✔	✔	–	✔	–	–	✔	–	✔	✔	–	–	✔
High, Red, & Leech	Toast Dream	✔	–	✔	✔	✔	✔	✔	✔	✔	–	✔	–	✔	–	✔	✔	–	–	✔

Features of Toaster Models

STRATEGY

Organize Information is a reading strategy. Use it to help you sort information you read.

READING COMPREHENSION

Group ideas as you read. That way, you get more out of what you read. Grouping ideas can help you see connections you may not otherwise see.

CRITICAL THINKING

As you read, put local information in places. This can make the reading piece more personal. Personal information often has more meaning for readers.

Reading Comprehension

Read the toaster buying guide information chart on page 109. Then answer the questions below.

1. **Organize Ideas:** Say you want to buy a four-slice toaster. You want to pay $50 or less. On page 109, put an **X** next to each toaster brand that could work. How many toasters did you mark? _____

2. **Group Ideas:** What are three main groups of information from the Toaster Buying Guide?

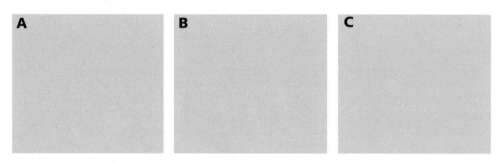

3. **Brainstorm:** What are three meals or dishes that could include toast?

   A _____

   B _____

   C _____

4. **Replace This:** The toaster features at the top of page 109 may be hard to understand. On your own paper, write or draw three toaster features.

Letters and Sounds Review

Circle the words with v/cv long vowel pattern. Put a box around the words with a v/v long vowel pattern. You will circle and box six words with more than two syllables.

1. area
2. brother
3. oasis
4. kitchen
5. open
6. violet
7. human
8. asleep
9. fuel
10. pilot

11. pencil
12. answer
13. alien
14. family
15. alias
16. almost
17. remain
18. tulip
19. biggest
20. later

21. inside
22. idea
23. event
24. hammer
25. famous
26. usual
27. honey
28. secret
29. recreate
30. happy

Language

Circle the correct words to make these sentences future tense.

1. Allen (wants, wanted, will want) to buy a new toaster.

2. He (likes, will like, liked) the four-slice toasters.

3. He (toasts, will toast, has toasted) more than two slices of bread at one time.

4. Ryan (ate, will eat, eats) toast every school morning.

5. He (made, makes, will make) toast five times a week.

6. Marisa (will plan, planned, plans) to toast bagels.

7. Sarah (will wonder, has wondered, wondered) if she can toast donuts.

8. Sarah (asked, asks, will ask) Allen if she can try his toaster.

9. Janell and Carlo (has asked, will ask, ask) their parents what they want for a gift.

10. Mr. and Mrs. Gomez (say, will say, have said) they (will want, wanted, want) a four-slice toaster.

LIFE SKILLS

Buying appliances can be a big decision. Some appliances cost a lot, such as stoves and refrigerators. Before you buy, make a list of important features.

Then find important information about each appliance. What are its safety features? What about repair history? How energy efficient is it?

Answering questions like these can help you decide which appliance to buy.

Think Further: Say you want to buy a toaster from the ones on page 109.

1. Choose a toaster that costs the least and still has the features you like.

Write the toaster's brand and model name. _____

_____

2. Below is a list of eight questions to ask before buying a small appliance such as a toaster. Answer each question for your toaster choice from Item 1 above.

■ What will I use this appliance for? _____

_____

■ Which features are most important to me? _____

_____

■ How many of my features does this appliance have?

_____

■ How often will I use this appliance?

_____

■ Where will I store it? _____

■ How much counter or storage space will this appliance need?

_____

■ Is this appliance easy to clean? Circle one   Yes   No   Don't know

■ Is this appliance easy to use? Circle one   Yes   No   Don't know

3. Based on your answers to Item 2 above, does the toaster you chose fit your needs?   Yes   No

Why or why not? _____

_____

_____

Lesson

22 BEFORE READING

Your Own Comparison Chart

LIFE SKILLS

A comparison chart shows how two or more things are alike and different. Information about government, people, history, or locations are often made into comparison charts.

Word Skills

Write a homophone for each word below. On your own paper, write a sentence using one or both of the words.

1. groan, _____

2. hair, _____

3. herd, _____

4. fowl, _____

5. pour, _____

6. no, _____

7. new, _____

8. pane, _____

9. road, _____

10. seem, _____

11. sense, _____

12. serial, _____

Use What You Know

Find and make a copy of a comparison chart. Look for comparison charts in magazines, books, catalogs, or on the Internet. Tape, staple, or glue the comparison chart to page 114. Then answer the questions below.

1. Have you ever used a comparison chart like this one? Circle one. Yes No

2. How many of your classmates used a comparison chart like yours? _____

Lesson 22

READING   Your Own Comparison Chart

Find a comparison chart. Look for comparison charts in magazines, books, catalogs, or on the Internet. Tape, staple, or glue your comparison chart to this page.

AFTER READING

Your Own Comparison Chart

Reading Comprehension

Read your comparison chart on page 114. Then answer the questions below.

1. **Organize Ideas:** Tell one way you could organize some information in the comparison chart to make it more meaningful for you.

   _____

   _____

   _____

2. **Group Ideas:** What are three main groups of information from your comparison chart?

A	B	C

3. **Brainstorm:** What are three ways the comparison chart could be helpful to someone?

   A _____

   B _____

   C _____

4. **Think Further:** Tell one thing you might understand or do differently because of reading the comparison chart.

   _____

   _____

   _____

Language Review

Fill in the blanks in the Past–Present–Future table below.

Past	Present	Future
fell	1. _____	2. _____
3. _____	buy	4. _____
5. _____	6. _____	will swim
sold	7. _____	8. _____
9. _____	cries	10. _____
11. _____	12. _____	will dive
13. _____	hop	14. _____

Writing

Say you want to open a kitchen appliance museum.

1. Use the space below to collect ideas for a short story about your kitchen appliance museum. If needed, use your own paper. Here are some ideas to get you started:

   ■ What appliances would you collect?
   ■ Where would you get appliances?
   ■ Where and how would you display them?
   ■ How would you let people know about your museum?
   ■ Why would people want to come to your museum?

2. On your own paper, write a short story based on your ideas. Write one or two paragraphs. When you are done, proofread your story.

3. Trade with a classmate and proofread each other's stories. Get your story back and make any changes. Write a final short story.

CAREER

Companies that make appliances keep coming up with new ideas. The new ideas help make people want to buy more appliances. This plan is true for most things you can buy.

Say you work for a toaster company. Think of a new toaster idea.

1. Make a drawing of your new toaster idea below.

2. Write a paragraph about your new toaster idea below.

_____

_____

_____

_____

_____

_____

_____

_____

_____

_____

_____

BEFORE READING

Today's Stock Market: March 11

PHONICS

The first vowel is long in both **v/cv** words and in **v/v** words.

VOCABULARY

abbreviation
a shortened word or phrase

closing
the end of the day

market
a place to buy and sell stock; the business of buying and selling something

previous
happening before something else

share
one of the equal parts of the stock of a company

stock
the shares in a company

trade
to exchange something in return for money or stocks

Letters and Sounds

Read the words in the box. Write the words where they belong below. For each word, look at the first syllable or the underlined syllable.

label Joseph ro<u>deo</u> science	donut ar<u>ea</u> cer<u>eal</u> sinus	prepare oasis cur<u>ious</u> Iowa	became depend exper<u>ience</u> gopher

v/cv	v/v
1. _____	9. _____
2. _____	10. _____
3. _____	11. _____
4. _____	12. _____
5. _____	13. _____
6. _____	14. _____
7. _____	15. _____
8. _____	16. _____

Use What You Know

Answer the questions below.

1. Have you read the stock market reports in the newspaper or on the Internet? Circle one.   Yes   No

2. Look in a newspaper for a stock market report. How much space is used for it?

   _____

3. Do you think stock market reports look interesting? Circle one.   Yes   No
   Why or why not?

   _____

READING   Today's Stock Market: March 11

Stock	Sym	Sales 100s	Last	Chg.
A				
AbbyLab	ABL	138711	5.67	−.03
Abcam	ABC	1624	9.09	−.02
AcneCo	ACE	14735	11.60	+.51
AcreHome	ACH	42474	35.53	+.83
AddlyOne	ADD	17526	27.80	+.36
Adfun	ADF	3109	7.42	+.08
AgProd	AGP	6107	42.52	−.26
AgRic	ARC	137201	4.10	+.99
Agsteen	AEN	1174	12.98	+.11
AirLow	ALW	8937	38.54	+.50
AirVacat	ARV	6792	14.04	−.10
AISLE	ILE	2198	17.46	+.46
Aivec Co	AVC	2998	2.89	+.02
Aizzel	AZZ	2795	8.04	+.14
Ajell	AJL	3572	14.05	+.77
AKA	AKA	8	9.69	+.01
Alder Inc.	LDR	28538	31.71	+.21
AlphaTech	APT	14966	43.08	+.16
ALPNB Cp	APB	6212	45.55	+.11
AMANZ	AMNZ	898	32.83	+.35
Amint	AMT	732	40.29	+1.22
Anople	ALE	9181	20.61	+.26
Anugg	ANG	133	7.97	+.12
AnoppLab	ANP	2217	19.23	+.43
Apant Co	APT	3482	22.20	+.35
AquaRed	AQR	15067	31.75	−.32
Arrow One	ARO	887	1.09	+.07
Arrow Co	ARW	11095	65.50	+.64
Asbro LTD	ASL	2813	36.65	+.10
Asdon Inc	ASD	14652	2.09	+.06
Attree	ATE	3069	45.05	−.60
Avapa	AVP	3213	57.7243	+.46

Stock	Sym	Sales 100s	Last	Chg.
B				
Bale Inc.	BAL	5504	13.94	+.26
Bane Five	BNF	118	1.58	−.02
Bappo	BPO	637	30.61	+.06
Barriston	BRT	610	26.39	+.52
Bartl	BRR	3320	30.97	+.45
BarReng	BRG	80	2.97	−.18
Bashot	BAO	26549	28.28	+.13
Bastrime	BSI	10113	61.69	+1.29
Battric	BRC	48756	21.78	+.08
Battuvle	BUV	3991	35.99	+.51
Bebru	BBU	28	3.50	+.01
Benstry	BNY	2990	14.04	+.24
Bettro	BTR	6989	27.58	+1.14
Binglish	BIH	2369	27.54	+.44
Bish Inc	BSH	3626	19.01	+.63
BootRun	BRN	314	5.47	+.45
Bozza Co	BZZ	933	35.85	−.11
BricksNow	BKN	1805	25.20	−.29
Brookshi	BOO	4152	25.67	+.15
Broshou	BRO	9210	24.82	+.02
Bupple	BUP	20392	46.20	−.37
Bylytle	BYT	22	18.07	+.05
C				
Cabro	CBR	2901	16.95	+.25
Caddingto	CAD	11433	4.00	+.41
Cadlo	CAL	810	11.97	+.09
Cagaron	CAG	58466	2.89	+.10
Cagemloc	CAC	1054	23.85	+.43
Capsten	CPS	3686	31.90	+.31
Captreige	CAP	10948	20.80	+1.99
Cas Andre	CAR	1653	30.66	+.32
Casgro Lu	CGL	2452	42.41	+.34
Cavren	CAV	644	34.11	+.47
CazzeeOne	CZZ	1130	20.99	+.58

Stock	Sym	Sales 100s	Last	Chg.
Cebro	CEB	652	36.06	+.55
CEB Tool	CET	20885	30.40	
Ceggiel	CGG		18.25	−.01
Celium	CEL	876	12.62	−.25
Cengree	CEG	577	35.23	−.08
CeNure	CEN	27827	58.20	+.16
CePree Lo	CPL	2324	24.33	+.15
Cerrenot	CRT	62	19.30	−.14
Cesteel	CST	607	8.86	+.43
Ceteure	CEU	9067	17.83	+.56
Cevary Co	CEV	74357	12.31	+.27
Chancelt	CHN	1176	9.59	+.13
Chapoolt	CHO	154	17.03	
Chenrie	CHR	1084	16.15	+.35
Chepplo	CPPL	3029	11.11	+.05
Cheptian	CTA	3660	6.15	−.01
Chessure	CSS	2261	9.18	+.03
Chethome	CEH	1699	26.93	+.32
Chipper	CHPR	1434	23.36	+.66
Chole	CHO	3622	32.75	+.54
Chozzen	COZ	4233	14.61	+.61
Ciddela	CDL	14572	47.47	+1.72
Cilla Clean	CLC	2744	22.37	+.67
Cippeeda	CIP	963	30.00	+.25
Cippeera	CPE	802	5.62	+.22
Cleone	CLE	2299	19.40	
Cleer Unit	CLU	1145	46.61	+.76
Clef Bro	CLF	2259	22.70	+.20
Clorer Co	CLO	2239	35.85	+1.50
Clufton	CLF	1817	14.30	+.38
Clyshel	CLY	5774	11.27	+.14
Conner	CON	15381	42.05	+.30
Coshean	COS	10381	34.49	+.55
CragEngin	CRE	583	13.25	+.04
Cytelian	CYT	45902	40.26	+.54

How to Read Stock Tables

Stock: Abbreviation for stock name

Sym: 3-letter abbreviation for stock name

Sales 100s: Number of **shares,** in hundreds, that **traded**. Add two zeroes to get total.

Last: Last sale price stock sold for, or **closing** price

Chg: Change between yesterday's closing price and the **previous** day's closing price

Today's Stock Market: March 11

LIFE SKILLS

Owning stock means that you own part of a company. If your company does well, your stock price may go up. However, if your company does poorly, your stock price may go down.

Reading Comprehension

Read the stock market report on page 119. Then answer the questions below.

1. **Study Text Features:** Why are the words and numbers in the stock market report so small?

   _____

   _____

2. **Study Pictures:** On March 1, Joe bought Acre Home Sites stock and Craig Engineering stock. He tracked the price of each stock for 10 days. Draw a single line in each graph that shows the pattern of the stock prices over this time.

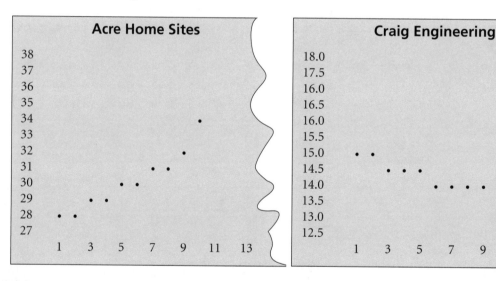

LIFE SKILLS

The oldest and largest stock market exchange in the United States is on Wall Street in New York City.

3. **Make a Chart:** Add the Acre Home Sites and Craig Engineering stock information from page 119 to the two graphs above. Add to the line you drew in Item 2.

4. **Author's Purpose:** Why do you think directions to read stock tables are at the bottom of stock market reports?

   _____

   _____

Letters and Sounds Review

Read the clues. Then write each v/cv or v/v word in the puzzle.

Clues
1. Count on, rely
2. Grass is a large part of a cow's _____
3. Spring flower
4. You write on this; made from trees
5. A prize or winning treat
6. Two singing together
7. Indian tent
8. To be the same as, often used in math
9. A place where books, magazines, and movies are kept

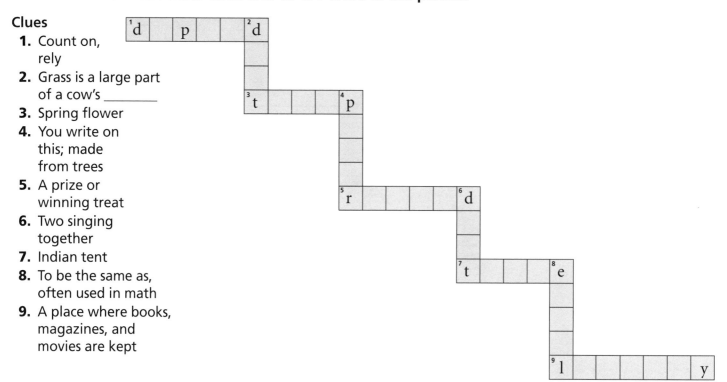

Language Review

Write sentences about stocks in the given tenses below. Be sure the subjects and verbs agree so the sentences sound right.

1. (present) _____

_____

2. (past) _____

_____

3. (future) _____

_____

4. (present) _____

_____

5. (past) _____

_____

6. (future) _____

_____

The stock market can be hard to understand. However, you do not have to understand everything to have some stock. You can buy stock through a stock broker who takes care of the paperwork. You can watch your stock go up or down by looking in the newspaper or on the Internet.

Life Skills Focus

Make Connections and Put in Order: Choose a stock from the newspaper or Internet. Keep track of your stock prices for the next five business days.

1. Write the days of the week and prices in the table below.

Name of Your Stock _____

Day of Week	Stock Price

2. Make a graph below. Put the prices and days of the week on your graph. Write a title for your graph. Write labels for the horizontal and the vertical lines. For help, see page 120.

Title: _____

Your Own Stock Market Report

WORD SKILLS

A **synonym** is a word with the same or nearly the same meaning as another word.

These four words—laugh, snicker, cackle, giggle—are synonyms. They mean about the same thing.

Word Skills

Write a synonym for each word below. On your own paper, write a sentence with a blank that you can fill in with either word.

1. little, _____

2. funny, _____

3. tall, _____

4. easy, _____

5. soft, _____

6. nibble, _____

7. frame, _____

8. road, _____

9. write, _____

10. company, _____

Use What You Know

Look in a newspaper or on the Internet for a stock market report. Tape, staple, or glue one page of a stock report to page 124. Then answer the questions below.

1. Where did you find your stock market report? _____

2. Where did your classmates find their stock market reports?

_____

_____

READING Your Own Stock Market Report

Look in a newspaper or on the Internet for a stock market report.
Tape, staple, or glue one page of a stock market report to this page.

Lesson **24** **AFTER READING**

Your Own Stock Market Report

STRATEGY

Study Text Features is a reading strategy you can use in almost everything you read.

Reading Comprehension

Read the stock market report on page 124. Then answer the questions below.

1. **Study Text Features:** Which text features below do you see in your stock report? Put an **X** beside each one.

   _____ **bold letters**   _____ *italics*   _____ **color**

   _____ bullets •   _____ type size   _____ centering

   _____ numbering   _____ <u>underline</u>

2. **Make Connections:** Find five companies you have heard of before. Write the companies below.

   A _____

   B _____

   C _____

   D _____

   E _____

3. **Make a Chart:** Choose five stocks. On your own paper, make a bar graph that shows the cost for each stock.

4. **Author's Purpose and Put Steps in Order:** How is the stock market report set up to help people find stocks?

   _____

   _____

   _____

Language Review

Fill in the blanks in the Past–Present–Future chart below.

Past	Present	Future
sang	1. _____	2. _____
3. _____	give	4. _____
5. _____	6. _____	will look
sank	7. _____	8. _____
9. _____	creeps	10. _____
11. _____	12. _____	will turn
13. _____	dances	14. _____

Writing

Make another entry in your journal about learning to read better. Thumb through pages 58 through 126 and look at the boxes. Choose at least two tips helpful to you. In your own words, tell why they are helpful. Read what you have written to make sure it says what you mean.

Career Connection

A hard part of a stockbroker's job is to find new customers.

1. Read the five main ways stockbrokers get new customers on the left below. Then draw a line to match each way with a cost.

Ways to get Customers	Costs
A Put ads in the newspaper	About 75¢ for each person
B Call people on the telephone	Free
C Send letters and postcards	$200 for five days
D Put on free classes	Ongoing monthly fee
E Be suggested by another customer	$300 for room rental, $100 for snacks, $30 for invitations and postage

2. People have different ways they like to work. How would you most like to get new customers? Circle your answer above.

3. Tell why you think you would like the way you circled in Item 2.

_____

_____

_____

_____

_____

SUMMARY OF SKILLS AND STRATEGIES

Look back at what you've learned in this book.

Reading Skills
You learned to:

- read words with letters that work together in different ways

- look at how words are built

- think about what you will read before you start to read

- sort and use information

- look at information in more than one way

Language and Writing Skills
You learned to:

- use correct capitalization and punctuation

- write facts and creative ideas

- sum up facts and ideas, and to use active voice

- use space wisely and write in a journal

- proofread what you write

Life and Career Skills
You learned how reading and writing relates to:

- planning personal finances and daily household chores

- being safe, making healthy choices, and traveling

- making plans, making choices, and getting along with people

- enjoying life and being involved in the world around you